To:

_____

With Love From:

_____

Seen

40 Days of Biblical Encouragement for Moms to Feel SEEN

Kendra Parks

SEEN

Scripture quotations marked (NIV) are taken from the Holy Bible, New International Version®, NIV®. Copyright © 1973, 1978, 1984, 2011 by Biblica, Inc.™ Used by permission of Zondervan. All rights reserved worldwide. www.zondervan.comThe "NIV" and "New International Version" are trademarks registered in the United States Patent and Trademark Office by Biblica, Inc.™

Scripture quotations marked (NASB) are taken from the NEW AMERICAN STANDARD BIBLE®, COPYRIGHT © 1960, 1962, 1963, 1968, 1971, 1972, 1973, 1975, 1977, 1995 by The Lockman Foundation. Used by permission.

Scripture quotations marked (NCV) are taken from the New Century Version®. Copyright © 2005 by Thomas Nelson. Used by permission. All rights reserved.

Scripture quotations marked (NLT) are taken from the Holy Bible, New Living Translation, copyright ©1996, 2004, 2015 by Tyndale House Foundation. Used by permission of Tyndale House Publishers, a Division of Tyndale House Ministries, Carol Stream, Illinois 60188. All rights reserved.

Scripture quotations marked (ESV) are from the ESV® Bible (The Holy Bible, English Standard Version®), copyright © 2001 by Crossway, a publishing ministry of Good News Publishers. Used by permission. All rights reserved."

ParksWrites Publishing
www.parkswrites.com

Copyright © 2020 by Kendra Parks

All rights reserved.
No part of this publication may be reproduced or transmitted in any form or by any means, electronic or mechanical, including photocopy, recording, or any information storage and retrieval system, without permission in writing from the publisher.
First paperback edition November 2020

Cover by Kendra and Jason Parks
ISBN 978-1-952967-05-4

For ALL of the moms who are determined to love and raise their sweet ones with hearts looking up. You are SEEN and are changing the world, dear friends.

I have no greater joy than to hear that my children are walking in the truth.

3 John 1:4 (NIV)

Table of Contents

Foreward: We all want to be **SEEN**.

Day 1: God Wants Your Heart..14

Day 2: Grace for YOU, Mama..18

Day 3: Practicing Faith..22

Day 4: Let's Re-Examine Blessings..26

Day 5: You are Never Alone..30

Day 6: Natural Rhythms..34

Day 7: Lay Down Your Life..38

Day 8: You Have Overcome the World..................................42

Day 9: Model Paul's Approach..46

Day 10: Perspective..50

Day 11: You Have Access to Supernatural Peace..................54

Day 12: Don't Fear the Quiet Spaces....................................58

Day 13: Don't Be Deceived...62

Day 14: May He Refresh Your Soul.......................................66

Day 15: Be a Shepherd, Mama..70

Day 16: God Knows. Find Comfort in That............................74

Day 17: Make Me Steady in the Face of Fear.......................78

Day 18: Hope: It's Yours for the Taking!...............................82

Day 19: Processing..86

Day 20: More Than We Can Conceive......................................90

Day 21: God Knows What is Coming Today.............................94

Day 22: He Remains Faithful..98

Day 23: Discouragement Will Come......................................102

Day 24: Delight in Suffering..106

Day 25: It's About Your Heart Attitude................................110

Day 26: In Whose Strength Do You Serve?...........................114

Day 27: Bookend Your Days with the Word........................118

Day 28: Ignore That Voice of Judgment, Sweet Mama!....122

Day 29: A Piece of Cake..126

Day 30: Are You Willing to Lose Comfort to be Closer to God?..130

Day 31: Hold Out for the Miracle.......................................134

Day 32: Just Say Yes..138

Day 33: With Leadership Comes Responsibility.................142

Day 34: Don't Miss His Voice in the Night..........................146

Day 35: Be Available...150

Day 36: Launch Your Children...154

Day 37: Sit Down and Teach Them, Mama..........................160

Day 38: Don't Drown Me Out. I Need Your Quiet. - God...164

Day 39: The Angel of the Lord is Terrifying.......................168

Day 40: Mother for Life...172

Foreward

We all want to be **SEEN**. By someone.

I started working on this devotional over a year ago, but God really laid the name of it on my heart at the end of 2019. I'm sharing this because I want you to know that **GOD. HAS. PLANS.** In fact, He prompted me to write that very phrase on a photo kitchen magnet at the start of 2020 and I kind of just shrugged my shoulders and said, "Yup!" I was completely clueless as to what was ahead. He knows and sees us and calls us to Himself regardless of what the enemy would throw our way. I didn't write these letters of encouragement knowing that they would release in the middle of a global pandemic in which we would be more confined to our homes and NEED to be SEEN more than ever before in our lives.

But God knows. And He sees. *He sees you.* He sees your family. He sees your situation. He sees your home. He sees your sorrows. He sees your joys. He sees your struggles. He sees you when you lose it. He sees you when you choose to let Him love you—and love through you.

I commented to my husband one Saturday that I just wanted more time with him, even though we had spent the entire day under the same roof. I wanted to be SEEN. He laughed and commented that we are always together…the children are just usually between us. As if to solidify his point, our three-year-old chose that moment to run up and stick a toy phone right in our faces to literally block our eyes from connecting. We both laughed. I wanted to be SEEN. Our three-year-old wanted to be SEEN. And our three-year-old won by demanding our attention be diverted to her. She was SEEN, and wearing a wide cheesy grin of victory.

Mama, if you've ever felt lost or invisible in a world that demands you become louder to be heard, to procure only beautiful images of your messy days, and share your philosophical interpretation of each day to feel worthy of being SEEN and understood, then this devotional is meant for you. It is filled up with reminders that you are SEEN.

SEEN without saying a word.
SEEN without taking a single picture.
SEEN by the God of the Universe.
SEEN and INVITED by God to sit at His feet.
SEEN and SUMMONED by Him to pour out your heart as He graciously pours out His forgiveness over your mistakes.
SEEN and HEARD by Your Heavenly Father as you question your qualifications and very existence…and He pours grace and TRUTH out over your heart.

Throughout this book, there is a blank space every day to write the ways in which you are SEEN by God. This is the space to write the eternal ways in which God views you today.

If you read this book in the evening, you can reflect on the ways God viewed you today. If you read this book in the morning, you can reflect on the day before or jot down a few intentional ways you plan to connect with your loved ones today to deepen your relationship with your husband, child, friend or co-worker who needs encouragement. This is the space to focus your heart on what is of eternal value. For example:

I am SEEN when I:

- Snuggled with Elle and read the same book over and over and over—she just needs the comfort of Mama's lap right now.

- Snuck a love note in J's laptop before he left for work and prayed for him throughout the day.

- Stayed off social media on purpose to keep my heart focused on presence with God and my family instead.

- Chose kindness, love and hugs over sarcasm with grumpy child today.

- Prayed over the kids before bed even though I wanted to skip it because I was exhausted.

- Stopped and talked with the houseless man outside the library and found out his favorite book is the Bible too. My whispered prayers for him were heard.

The Discipling Point:

This section is about bringing what you are learning to your kids. Don't feel like you must follow these exactly. They are simply ideas for how you might speak the truths that God is writing onto your heart into your childrens' hearts. Consider how the Spirit moves you to share what you learn at some point that day. This might not happen every day, but my hope is that these discipling points remind you of your capacity to steward God's work in *your* heart into your people's lives. Your learning and your actions affect those around you. Share what He is teaching you.

God's Whispers:

Write what God is whispering to you today…a daily reminder to listen for His voice.

A Note about Writing Verses:

Please note that I have not written out the verses at the start of each day on purpose, because I believe God's Word is powerful and I will do anything to encourage you to crack it open. My words are mere human words, but His Words, well, they hold supernatural power. I pray that writing His Living Words in your translation of choice helps cement them to your memory as well.

These **SEEN**-by-God moments and whispers from Him that you write out are the things that your Christian walk through life is really about…written to refocus your heart on the eternal. **I pray that after 40 days of focusing on these eternally significant moments in your life, that you will look back and SEE God deeply at work within your life, your heart and the family that He has authored, and that you will KNOW that you are SEEN.** He has amazing plans for your family!

Love to you, Sweet Mama, from our Lord and Savior Jesus Christ!

Kendra

Behold, children are a gift of the LORD,
The fruit of the womb is a reward.

Psalm 127:3 (NASB)

Day 1

Pray for wisdom and read: **Psalm 143**

_____

_____

Psalm 143:8

God Wants Your Heart

Early on in my idealism of motherhood, I felt like I was less-than if I didn't begin my days with a cup of tea and God's Word…waking before my sweet ones to spend time with my heavenly Father. I quickly discovered this time would not exist in our household as we found ourselves loving colicky babies with endless ear infections and reflux and allergies and sleep problems and some needs that meant those early morning times just were not going to be consistent.

And God showed me something. He showed me that He just wanted my heart. He SAW me. He SAW my love of our children and He blessed my pursuit of Him. My faith grew stronger through the challenging nights as I poured out my heart to Him, and He showed me that I could pursue Him at any time of the day or night.

Mama, if you're feeling like you are failing because your

days are not consistent and your children aren't clockwork in their sleep habits, God wants your heart. Mama, if your babes are on a clockwork schedule and you can pick your perfect time slot for bible study, God wants your heart. Mama, if you are a mama-in-waiting—you aren't yet holding a babe in your arms, but you are pleading and praying for one—God wants your heart.

Keep pursuing God. Leave your Bible open in a place in your home that you walk past a gazillion times a day. Grab morsels of wisdom as you can in this season. Psalm 143:8 was a verse that God led me to night after night as I walked fussy babes around our home, dark with shadows, and yet lit up by my heavenly Father.

Pray over your babe whether he/she is in your arms yet or not. Take moments to shut off your phone and sit quietly before your Savior. He is always there. Waiting for you to turn to Him. He loves you, precious daughter of His! And He has PLANS for you. You just need to look back at Him and give Him your heart…and wait for Him to speak. He will.

Discipling Point:

Set yourself up for success today in studying God's Word. Have your older kids help you find your Bible and set it in a well-trafficked area of your home or where you tend to calm your precious babe in the middle of the night. Show them by example that you are serious about staying rooted in God's Word. I put mine on a stand that used to be mainly for seasonal decor. Consider purchasing a battery-operated timer candle to place next to it. Set the timer to turn on in the middle of the night or early morning when your babe tends to wake you. May the light draw you into the LIGHT of God's Word.

I am SEEN when I:

God's Whispers:

Prayer

Jesus, thank you for coming to be the LIGHT of the world. Thank you for lighting my way. Thank you for your constant presence through your Holy Spirit. Pull me closer to you as I read your living Word. I long to grow in my faith and relationship with you to live a life that glorifies our Father in heaven.
Amen.

My Prayers:

Let the morning bring me word of your unfailing love, for I have put my trust in You.

Psalm 143:8 (NIV)

Day 2

Pray for wisdom and read: **1 John 1**

_____

_____

1 John 1:9

Grace for YOU, Mama

I'm not sure you have had them, but I certainly have. The days where I fall into bed asking God not to let my kids remember me as "that mom" today. And by "that mom," I mean the overwhelmed, tired, yelling mom who somehow snuck into my body and took my sweet self hostage today, of course.

If you're reading this through tears because you just went on a rant and stomped through the house asking your kids why they can't just confine their legos to one room after stepping on those razor-sharp pieces of plastic creativity while swiping two more out of your teething toddlers' bulging cheeks (not writing from personal experience here at all, by the way)? Grace and Jesus, sweet Mama.

This is why Jesus came. I am convinced that motherhood has the opportunity to carve out our humility like no other occupation can. Ask and accept Jesus' forgiveness. We all mess up. The beauty of being a Christian mom is that we have forgiveness. To receive, and also to humbly request from the precious little hearts we have been entrusted with. My kids know about forgiveness at an early age mostly because of MY mistakes.

Mamas, you have the opportunity to model healthy communication right within the walls of your home when you choose to walk your children through apologizing and asking for forgiveness. And if and when they genuinely offer you or a sibling their forgiveness? Soak it in, and praise Jesus for His work in your family and in each of your hearts.

Discipling Point:

Be willing to ask your kids for forgiveness when you lose it, Mama. Take a deep breath and realize you are teaching them an incredible life-changing lesson at the very core of your faith. If we don't live out forgiveness through Jesus, we don't have faith. And when your kids make a mistake? Help them ask for forgiveness, and cover them with the same grace you long to receive when you mess up. Remind them who this Jesus you talk about is and is all about.

I am SEEN when I:

-
-
-
-
-

God's Whispers:

Prayer

God, please forgive me for _____. Thank you for your grace and forgiveness. Thank you that regardless of how much I mess up, your mercies and love are always available to me if I confess my sin to you. Please help me to do better next time. Help me to be more patient and loving as you are with me.
Amen.

My Prayers:

If we confess our sins, he is faithful and just and will forgive us our sins and purify us from all unrighteousness.

1 John 1:9 (NIV)

Pray for wisdom and read: **Philippians 4:1-9, 1 Thessalonians 5:16-18**

Philippians 4:9

Practicing Faith

I'm a firm believer that practice doesn't make perfect. I am under no illusion that perfection lives on this earth. Jesus was perfect. We are not, nor were we created to be. As 1 John 1:8 (NIV) states,

If we claim to be without sin, we deceive ourselves and the truth is not in us.

Claiming perfection nullifies our need for Jesus.

But regular practice DOES create a training ground for our kids to learn and develop. I'm not just talking about practicing piano, handwriting, math facts, dance or basketball. I'm talking about practicing faith. To practice praying, my kids pray before breakfast, lunch and dinner. Even our two-year-old prays. Not because I sit down and tell him how to pray, but because three times each day, he hears one of his siblings or his mom or dad pray aloud.

It's pretty basic, Mama. This was his prayer: "Thank you God for this beautiful day. Thank you for this food. Please help sister to get over her crying sickness through the night so mom and dad can sleep."

Seriously, the things brilliant little minds come up with to tack onto the end of their prayers is worth a book in itself.

One of my older kiddos asked me recently why he hadn't heard God's voice. I asked him when he last sat quietly somewhere by himself and listened. He disappeared and returned 2.3 minutes later saying he heard nothing. I explained that he might need to regularly spend quiet time with God to hear His whispers. And what did he say? "Ah, like you do, right?" They are watching you, Mama. Model well.

So today, I encourage you to think about the spiritual "practicing" you are opening up for your kids to explore. Be consistent in your faith training and then step back and watch God move in your kiddos' hearts!

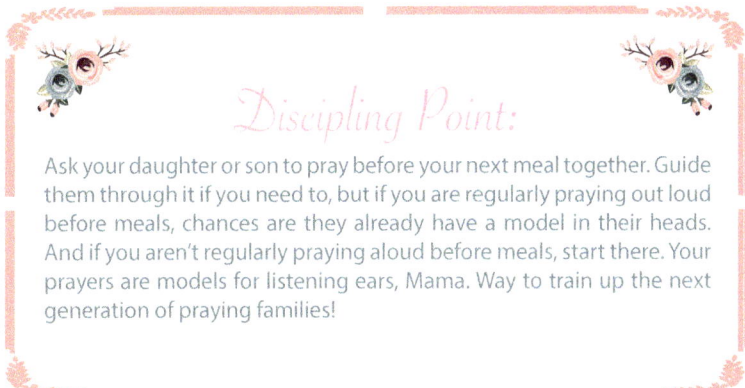

Discipling Point:

Ask your daughter or son to pray before your next meal together. Guide them through it if you need to, but if you are regularly praying out loud before meals, chances are they already have a model in their heads. And if you aren't regularly praying aloud before meals, start there. Your prayers are models for listening ears, Mama. Way to train up the next generation of praying families!

I am SEEN when I:

-
-
-
-
-

God's Whispers:

Prayer

God, please give me wisdom and insight as I teach my kids about you. Open all of our hearts to know you more—to please you, knowing that we are SEEN by you. Help me to consistently model my faith well. We love you and praise you for the gift it is to know you every day.
Amen.

My Prayers:

Whatever you have learned or received or heard from me, or seen in me—put it into practice. And the God of peace will be with you.

Philippians 4:9 (NIV)

Day 4

Pray for wisdom and read: **Luke 6:20-38, Matthew 5:1-12**

Luke 6:20b-23a

Let's Re-Examine Blessings

God's word has a way of turning the world's definitions upside-down, doesn't it? Blessings according to God's Word are no different.

My first thought is to say I am blessed when bills are paid or when we have a pleasant vacation away as a family.

But take a moment to read Luke 6:20-23 and Matthew 5:3-10. According to the world, the situations listed in these Scripture passages are NOT the moments when the average person would shout, "I am BLESSED!!!"

For example:

"Goodness, I am poor and BLESSED because of it!!!"
"I am so BLESSED to be a weeping mess right now!!!"

But God's wisdom prevails once more and sheds an eternal light on our finite circumstances. Because our earthly lives are finite. And while this is tough to wrap our selfish human minds around, it is an important concept to understand in light of other verses in Scripture that discuss how we will be blessed.

> *Praise be to the God and Father of our Lord Jesus Christ, who has blessed us in the heavenly realms with every spiritual blessing in Christ.*
> Ephesians 1:3 (NIV)

We must gaze past our finite expectations to see God's blessings in our lives. Our blessings that we receive when we pursue righteousness are not of this world. They are eternal.

 *Discipling Point:*

Ask your kids what they think a blessing is. Make a list with them of worldly blessings vs. eternal blessings based on these verses. Also, pray today about what you can do together WITH your children this week that will have eternal consequences that glorify God. Keep your eyes open for opportunities, Mama. Let God's Spirit move you.

I am SEEN when I:

God's Whispers:

Prayer

Dear God, help me to see and accept your blessings in my life. I thank you for them. Remind me of your promise in Jeremiah 29:11—that as your daughter, you plan to prosper me and not to harm me. Your plans are to give me hope and a future. Please open my eyes to see my life and my current situations with your eternal perspective. Help me to understand what I can, and to trust you with what I cannot.
Amen.

My Prayers:

Blessed are you who are poor, for yours is the kingdom of God.
Blessed are you who hunger now, for you shall be satisfied.
Blessed are you who weep now, for you shall laugh.
Blessed are you when men hate you, and ostracize you, and insult you, and scorn your name as evil, for the sake of the Son of Man.
Be glad in that day and leap for joy, for behold, your reward is great in heaven.

Luke 6:20b-23a (NASB)

Day 5

Pray for wisdom and read: **Matthew 28:1-20**

_____

_____

Matthew 28:20

You are Never Alone

God goes with you today, sweet one. Wherever you are, whatever is weighing heavy on your heart, God is WITH you. Lean into Him as you remember to today, and don't try to do life on your own!

Opposite of the world's mantra that "you can do this," the Christian response should be, "you can't do this…but with God, you can."

If it feels like a herculean effort to force a smile on your face today, pray for God to bring you joy that will place it there.

If you can't see an end to your pain today, ask God to renew your hope for healing.

If you feel alone and like no one cares about you, it's Satan hissing lies in your ear. Re-read the verse above, dear one.

If you can't muster an ounce of strength to do your daily work, pray for God's strength to hold you up and carry you through it.

And don't be upset if your answer doesn't come right away. Instead, look for it today, because it WILL come. And when it does, look up and thank God for it.

Remember that when you feel joy in the midst of sorrow, uncertainty, pain and isolation, it HAS to be supernatural. If you have accepted Jesus Christ as your Savior, then God's Spirit is in you, precious one. He. Is. With. You.

He SEES you and longs for you to acknowledge Him and His presence in your life. Choose to SEE Him today. Look up and SEE that He is good.

Taste and see that the LORD is good;
blessed is the one who takes refuge in him.
Psalm 34:8 (NIV)

Discipling Point:

Choose today to envision your kids as adults. Imagine how they will reflect on their childhood experience and the issues that might still be a struggle for them. Is there a way today that you can speak into those places in their hearts with the hope of Jesus? Speak and stockpile God's loving truths into your kids' hearts today so that they will hear them years from now when they are having a heavy-hearted day. Remind them that God is with them to the very end of the age.

I am SEEN when I:

-
-
-
-
-

God's Whispers:

Prayer

God, thank you that I am never alone. Thank you that YOU go with me everywhere I go. Thank you that you are with me NOW. Thank you that your Spirit is in me as your Word says in 2 Corinthians 1:22. I claim Your presence in my heart and life and trust you to carry me today. I cannot do this day alone. Thank you, Jesus. Amen.

My Prayers:

And surely I am with you always, to the very end of the age.

Matthew 28:20 (NIV)

Day 6

Pray for wisdom and read: **Matthew 11:25-30; Ecclesiastes 3:1-22**

Matthew 11:28-30

Natural Rhythms

I was lying next to my boys in their room recently as they were falling asleep, and I was listening intently to nature's "sound machine" through the open window. It was so calming and rhythmic with the crickets and occasional hooting owl in the woods.

It made me think of how much we miss out on by living inside of man-made structures. It reminded me of how God designed us and designed all of nature with rhythms of quiet, calm and rest as well as energetic sunny, bird-singing, deer-springing days.

Today, take note of nature's rhythms and think about your own daily rhythms. Do you have a balance of rainy/restful moments, sunny/playful moments, and even dreary/contemplative moments? If not, ask God today to give you a vision for a better daily rhythm and jot down some ideas to enact that which He presses onto your heart.

And before you are tempted to google "daily rhythms," remember that your family's daily rhythms will be unique and unlike other families'.

Your kids and your family dynamics are specially crafted by God, so go to Him first for inspiration, Mama. He sees you and your family's needs. Get quiet before Him and listen for His wisdom to lead your family into rhythms that honor Him with your days.

> *The thief comes only to steal and kill and destroy;*
> *I have come that they may have life, and have it to the full.*
> John 10:10 (NIV)

Let God fill your days with rhythmic life which is eternally satisfying.

Discipling Point:

Are you looking for more rest in your day? Take 30 minutes today to brew and share some tea and a snack. Talk, look up some jokes or read a book aloud with your kids. My kids all love blueberry, peach and chamomile herbal teas (carefully cooled with ice cubes of course)! Taking 15-20 minutes to sip tea and read a good book aloud, giggle through "would-you-rather" questions, or listen to some music with my kids (older kids too!) is a regular game/mood changer in our home.

I am SEEN when I:

God's Whispers:

Prayer

Thank you God for your natural model of rhythms in your Creation. Inspire my heart and mind to create a home that reflects daily rhythms that best balance our family's hearts and minds to stay focused on YOU. I love you and praise you for all of the different ways you have created me to feel and live and love. It is such an honor to be your beautiful creation.
Amen.

My Prayers:

Come to Me, all who are weary and heavy-laden, and I will give you rest. Take My yoke upon you and learn from Me, for I am gentle and humble in heart, and you will find rest for your souls. For My yoke is easy and My burden is light.

Matthew 11:28-30 (NASB)

Day 7

Pray for wisdom and read: **1 John 3**

_____

_____

1 John 3:16

Lay Down Your Life

Every time I rediscover the verse above, I am moved at the parallel Scripture address of John 3:16 (NIV).

For God so loved the world that he gave his one and only Son, that whoever believes in him shall not perish but have eternal life.

If love is about laying our lives down for one another, then how did you love in the last hour? Did you give up a night of sleep to love on a sweet baby that was cutting new molars? Did you give the last cookie to your son after lunch? Did you sit and cuddle your sick 8-year-old and let the laundry sit knowing it means a later night for you? Sometimes we think this verse only works in those big things we do that others see, but I want to encourage you to think about the hidden moments today. I am always reminding my kids that what we do in the hidden places of life, where people don't see our choices, is WHO WE ARE. If we are making good choices behind closed doors, then we will not be swayed by the amount of 'likes' we get when we give or serve those around us. We will be serving and loving out of a pure place. A place quiet enough to hear God's voice direct us rather than only doing good to receive praise from the world.

> *But when you give to the needy, do not let your left hand know what your right hand is doing, so that your giving may be in secret. Then your Father, who sees what is done in secret, will reward you.*
> Matthew 6:3-4 (NIV)

Find ways to love in the hidden things you do today. Those moments when you take deep breaths rather than yell at your kids. The moment when you are tired and just want some quiet, yet your 3-year-old skipped his nap and is bouncing off the walls... and you choose to make a cup of coffee or tea and read yet another book to him or run around outside with him to get those wild wiggles out. God sees your extra effort and love, Mama. When you roll with the crazy and laugh rather than lose it. When you shake your head and realize you only get this day once and choose to be present with your child rather than zone out with a screen. God sees the extra effort it takes, Mama. This is laying your life down. God is with you, sweet one. He will give you everything you need to lay yourself down and LOVE through each moment today. Keep going. God's love working through you is changing the world.

Discipling Point:

Talk to your kiddos today about what it means to lay our lives down for one another. It may look like giving their sibling the fuller-looking cup of juice in the morning or holding the door for someone else to go first when going outside. It may look like selling handmade items or toys to raise money for someone in need. You know your kiddos. Give examples that speak to their hearts, sweet Mama. Trust that God made you their Mama for a reason and will give you wisdom to speak the right words.

I am SEEN when I:

-
-
-
-
-

God's Whispers:

Prayer

God, thank you so much for sending Jesus into the world for me—for giving up your precious Son to take the place of my sin and mess. Today please guide me in how I can live out of a sacrificial place. May my sacrificial living not be rooted in bitterness. Instead, please fill my heart with such joy and love from you that my sacrifice comes from a pure place. I love you and long for more of you. Amen.

My Prayers:

This is how we know what love is: Jesus Christ laid down his life for us. And we ought to lay down our lives for our brothers and sisters.

1 John 3:16 (NIV)

Day 8

Pray for wisdom and read: **1 John 5:1-12; Colossians 3:1-17**

1 John 5:4

Colossians 3:17

You have Overcome the World

Sometimes in life there is a situation or relationship that we just aren't going to be able to solve. But guess what? We are in control of our *attitude* toward that situation or relationship.

We can become a victim and claim defeat or we can seek Scripture and realize that as Believers, we can claim victory—for Scripture says that we have overcome the world!

Well that's great I think, but what about that unsettled situation? That's where the Colossians verses come in. God doesn't promise immediate answers to our problems, but when we search His Living Word, we can find direct commands as to how to lead our daily lives. Whatever we do, whatever we say, we are to do it with our "new self" in Jesus' name, thanking God. This is our guidance to walking through a Godly response to a challenging situation.

I've also found that sometimes that voice inside of me that feels disgruntled, is the part of me that needs to STAND UP for what God is pressing on my heart. And that standing up? Well, it often looks like humbly bowing my head and asking for forgiveness and listening better. Once I do what I feel Him calling me to do, I feel at peace again.

You are seen, Mama. Listen, obey His voice, and overcome and claim victory through Jesus, because you are a daughter of the Lord Most High.

Praise Him and give Him thanks today!

Discipling Point:

As much as we wish to shield our kids from pain, there will be hardships in this world they will walk through that are heart-shattering. Raise them as the adults they are growing into, by sharing the wisdom you are learning with them. When they are feeling defeated by a situation, remind them that they are overcomers by knowing God, and that they win when they respond to their challenge in a way that honors God. And give thanks to God together when you see victory!

I am SEEN when I:

*
*
*
*
*

God's Whispers:

Prayer

God, I humbly bow to you today and praise you for the honor it is to know you and be your child. Through you, I have overcome this world, and I pray that you remind me of this today. Remind me that you see me as an over-comer when others in this world tell me otherwise. Thank you for your love and belief in me. I love you. Amen.

My Prayers:

For everyone born of God overcomes the world.

1 John 5:4 (NIV)

And whatever you do, whether in word or deed, do it all in the name of the Lord Jesus, giving thanks to God the Father through him.

Colossians 3:17 (NIV)

Day 9

Pray for wisdom and read: **Philippians 4**

_____

_____

Philippians 4:8

Model Paul's Approach

Philippians 4 is one of my favorite passages in the Bible. I keep returning to Paul's words for the direction, encouragement and hopeful promises that keep me focused on the Gospel-focused life I long to live out. There is the reminder to pray with thanks to replace my worrying, words to think on to still my swirling mind, and promises of peace that exceed anything I can understand.

In our children's world today, there are a lot of options. When I was a child, we watched whatever cartoon was scheduled for the time slot we had to watch a show (yup, I'm that ancient). Now there are thousands of episodes of children's shows available at a finger's touch. As our family makes choices about what to watch, Paul's list of what to think on guides our decisions.

If you notice your child's behavior altering in a negative way after watching certain shows, then as the parent, guess what? You have permission to guide their choices to a new show.

Paul's wisdom not only applies to our children's television choices. When we as mothers are consuming negative media or spending too much time following online figures rather than God's Word, our choices and behavior will be negatively altered. And likewise, when we are daily spending time in God's Word and listening to wisdom and music that points our hearts up to God, our daily attitudes and choices for our families will be eternally impacted.

Model Paul's approach to protecting the gift of your mind that God has entrusted you with. I guarantee that choosing His Word over the world's entertainment offerings will bring you peace and hopeful assurance every time.

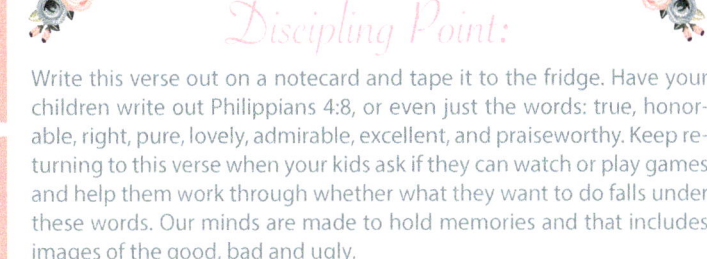

Discipling Point:

Write this verse out on a notecard and tape it to the fridge. Have your children write out Philippians 4:8, or even just the words: true, honorable, right, pure, lovely, admirable, excellent, and praiseworthy. Keep returning to this verse when your kids ask if they can watch or play games and help them work through whether what they want to do falls under these words. Our minds are made to hold memories and that includes images of the good, bad and ugly.

I am SEEN when I:

-
-
-
-
-

God's Whispers:

Prayer

Thank you God, for the guidance that you leave us through your Living Word. Give us endurance as parents to keep stepping up and standing up to the world's standards and weighing them with your standards. Remind us that we have been entrusted with our kids' hearts. We long to honor you by teaching and guiding them as they grow and learn to make good choices on their own.
Amen.

My Prayers:

Finally, brothers and sisters, whatever is true, whatever is noble, whatever is right, whatever is pure, whatever is lovely, whatever is admirable—if anything is excellent or praiseworthy—think about such things.

Philippians 4:8 (NIV)

Day 10

Pray for wisdom and read: **Isaiah 66:1-10**

Isaiah 66:9a (NCV)

Perspective

Any time our family goes for a walk down our street, I love breathing in the fresh air and listening to nature's orchestra: the varying bird songs, the rustling leaves tumbling around on the ground, the chattering squirrels…and I smile at the familiar timeless sound of our neighbor's wind chime spilling even more lovely tones into the air.

Perspective is everything though. While I love the sound of that chime on a family walk at three o'clock in the afternoon, the same chime wildly "singing" during a rainstorm in the middle of the night when I am trying to sleep suddenly becomes obnoxious.

Remember, today, when you begin to view your circumstances in a negative light, that maybe God views them differently. Ask Him for clarity and His eternal perspective. And remember that He is always working good for you, dear one. Perhaps the pain you are experiencing right now is actually birthing something new and beautiful in your life!

I can look back now at heart-wrenching challenges in my life, like the death of my father on the morning my daughter was born, and see God's hand preparing me for challenges I face now. Likewise, I understand that my current trials may be preparation for something in the future. His ways are higher than mine and His timing is beyond my comprehension.

> But do not let this one fact escape your notice, beloved, that with the Lord one day is like a thousand years, and a thousand years like one day.
>
> 2 Peter 3:8 (NASB)

Choose to trust God's plans and His timing for you and your family today. If He can turn the death of His only precious Son into the redemptive beauty of the christian life, then I'm willing to trust Him with my finite worldly pain.

Discipling Point:

Show your children the reverse side of a cross-stitch pattern or tapestry. Find a picture online if you need to, or you can also use the reverse side of a rug or piece of clothing that looks messy on one side but neat on the other side. Speak to your little ones about how sometimes when all we see is the mess, God sees the beauty on the other side.

I am SEEN when I:

-
-
-
-
-

God's Whispers:

Prayer

Heavenly Father, I praise you today that you have an eternal perspective on my circumstances. I'm trusting today that my view is clouded and that You have intentional plans in mind for my life even as I sit overwhelmed. Please open my mind and heart to see with your eyes and a heaven-focused perspective, that I may feel hopeful for all that you have in store for me.
Thank you, Jesus.
Amen.

My Prayers:

"I will not cause pain without allowing something new to be born," says the Lord.
Isaiah 66:9a (NCV)

Day 11

Pray for wisdom and read: **1 John 5:1-12; Exodus 3:1-12**

Exodus 3:12

You Have Access to Supernatural Peace

1 John 5:1-4 tells us that when we believe that Jesus Christ is God's Son, we become a child of God and that every child of God overcomes this world. If you believe in Jesus Christ, you overcome this world through your faith. Jesus says we will have trouble in this world (John 16:33), but that we have peace through Him because He has overcome the world.

What this reminds me today is that regardless of the struggle I find myself swirling in, I have access to the peace of Jesus IN THE MIDST of it. Not just when the struggle passes, but right in the chaos of the storm.

The key to that peace is my mindset. If I'm staring right at the storm, I can't see anything around me and I feel anxiously under attack. If I look up, Jesus can refresh my perspective and remind me that He is with me. The God who created the world and the endless galaxies beyond our own is with me (Exodus 3:12).

God is with us through incoming endless medical bills and unemployment. God is with us through the numbing and heart-wrenching and accepting stages of grief and loss. God is with us through an ungrateful, hurting child's attacks. God is with us when everyone else walks away. God is with us through a broken marriage. God is with us through that unspoken illness or addiction that is taking over our life. God is with us when terrifying illnesses loom all around us and everything we've known as "normal" is no more. God is with me—and YOU—right now.

Take a deep breath, and accept His presence.

Discipling Point:

One of my kiddos has a lot of fear before bed about various scary monsters that invade his mind. I couldn't get his anxious heart calmed - not with night lights, magic monster spray, talking, listening, happy pictures or uplifting music. Nothing worked until I finally prayed a prayer over him including the part that the God who created him, me, the universe, stars, planets and beyond…says not to fear, for He is with us. This child has accepted Christ in his heart, so I was able to claim that out loud for him to remind him that He holds that powerful Creator who has overcome this world in his heart and thus has no need to fear. And you know what? I felt his nervous heart relax and received a huge hug followed by sleep shortly after. This prayer has been requested each night. Don't underestimate your power to pray over your children! Don't worry about what you say, trust the Spirit in YOU to give you the words your child needs. God made you your kiddos' mama for a reason. Trust Him to guide you in calming your kids' hearts before you reach for an article on your phone with "proven methods." Your God was around way before Google, sweet Mama.

I am SEEN when I:

God's Whispers:

Prayer

God, thank you for your presence. Thank you for your peace. I pray for your peace now as I lay my day, my marriage, my family, my fears, and my relationships before you. Please cover my heart with your peace as I step forward. Calm my heart and keep me looking up to YOU rather than the messiness and loud world around me. What a gift it is to have your Spirit in me. Keep guiding my heart to line up with your own. Amen.

My Prayers:

And the LORD answered, "My presence will go with you, and I will give you rest."

Exodus 3:12

Day 12

Pray for wisdom and read: **Ecclesiastes 5:1-9**

Ecclesiastes 5:2

Don't Fear the Quiet Spaces

Sometimes I approach God more with a reporting (or social media posting) mentality rather than a relational mindset. But rather than bowing my head and pouring out my own words and thoughts and aches and requests *at* Him, I must remember my place.

The God of the Universe has invited me to bow before Him. If I were to enter into an earthly King and Queen's presence, would I dare jump right into complaining and listing my grievances with the world around me? How much more must I approach God with a humble heart, listening first for His voice to invite me into conversation with Him. And when He does invite me to spill my heart out to Him, may I realize the honor it is to cry out to my eternal God and Father.

Along with this realization comes the skill of active listening. Sometimes I wonder how long I am to listen for His voice.

Sometimes I'm willing to wait, and out of the stillness and the quiet, He speaks and I hear. Other times, I am impatient and certain I miss out on what He longs to speak to my needy heart. Still other times, I wait in the quiet, and though I hear no words, my soul feels an overwhelming peace and calm that only comes supernaturally. Our God works in many more ways than just words, dear ones. Don't be afraid of the quiet.

As a musician, I am aware of the power of the "pause"… the increased impact of a loud cymbal crash after a decrescendo and a pause. The power of the "pause" is important in other areas of life as well. As a storyteller to my children, my pauses enhance any dramatic expressions I attempt. So may it be with your "pauses" before your God and Maker. May your regular life "pauses" enhance your everyday walk with the Lord.

Discipling Point:

Play a game of 'sound' hide-and-seek. We use a toy turtle that plays music, but you could use a small portable speaker or a crib toy that plays music. Get creative! Now have your kids hide their eyes and count in one place while you find a secret place to hide the sound-making toy/speaker. Your kids have to stay quiet (score, right?!) and listen really carefully to find it. My youngest kids love this game! It also opens up the chance for you to talk to them about how important it is to get quiet and learn to listen for God's voice in their lives. Pair this game with the story of Samuel in their Bible.

I am SEEN when I:

-
-
-
-
-

God's Whispers:

Prayer

God, I humbly bow before you now and ask that you would quiet my mind and my words so I can hear your words and feel your presence…(listen for His whispers)…I love you and long to know more of you.
Amen.

My Prayers:

"Do not be quick with your mouth, do not be hasty in your heart to utter anything before God. God is in heaven and you are on earth, so let your words be few."

Ecclesiastes 5:2

Day 13

Pray for wisdom and read: **Matthew 24:1-14; 1 Corinthians 16:13; 1 Peter 5:6-11**

Matthew 24:4-5

Don't Be Deceived

"It's hailing!" said one of my little ones recently, looking out our front picture window at what looked like mini inch-long ice swords falling to the ground before our eyes. It did indeed appear to be ice falling from the sky, and it continued to fall fairly rhythmically for several minutes. But it looked just a little "off." The hail we usually see looked like little balls of ice, not mini spears of ice. Upon further investigation as my husband went outside to prepare for a run, wondering if the hail would end, he declared that it was not actually hail, but ice chunks melting from the many trees around us and being blown down by the wind that blustery morning.

We had been fooled. God's Word warns us to watch out for those trying to deceive us. "To deceive" is defined as causing someone to believe something that is not true, typically in order to gain some personal advantage.

Are you being deceived in your walk with God? Is there someone or something that has entered into your faith walk that doesn't belong there? Are you following a person more than you're following God? Are you following a feed of feel-good sayings or pulling out your Bible and reading the truth straight from its pages?

> *All your words are true;*
> *all your righteous laws are eternal.*
> Psalm 119:160 (NIV)

Pull out your Bible and underline the verse above. Find a Bible reading plan or choose a book of the Bible to read through. Read a chapter a day. You don't have to wait until January 1 to begin reading God's Word. It's already been released, sweet one! Open it up, and watch Him work in your life! You will never regret studying His Word.

Discipling Point:

Ask your child if God is mentioned in any of the shows or books they are watching or reading. Let this spur a conversation about where we learn how we are to live. Direct their hearts to God's Word by sharing a verse that spoke to you in your quiet time today. Never underestimate God's ability to use these small intentional moments to root His Word into your children's hearts. This also is great accountablity to your own time with the Lord. He has a way of sealing spiritual moments into your children's hearts on a spiritual level that other memories cannot match, Mama. Direct them to the truth of God's Word today.

I am SEEN when I:

-
-
-
-
-

God's Whispers:

Prayer

God, please open my eyes to your truths. Help me to differentiate between your truths and the lies of this world. Satan wants to pull me away from you, but I long to draw closer to you. Please pull me in close. Keep me daily opening your Word and help me to understand it. Help me to hear and feel your heart—may my heart beat as one with yours.
Amen.

My Prayers:

Jesus answered: "Watch out that no one deceives you. For many will come in my name, claiming, 'I am the Messiah,' and will deceive many."

Matthew 24:4-5 (NIV)

Day 14

Pray for wisdom and read: **Psalm 23**

Psalm 23:3

May He Refresh Your Soul

I found myself soaking in the peace-filled promises of this Psalm one morning while pregnant, enduring sleepless nights with a 10-month-old and setting up doctor's appointments for two other sick children in our house.

These words soothed my heart as I leaned into God's truths to find much-needed soul-rest and peace. In a world that pushes expectations beyond our human capacity many days, there is always a place ready for us to retreat to—the arms and shelter of our Mighty God and Shepherd.

If you're feeling worn out today, take a moment to refresh your heart with the promises of Psalm 23. This is a Psalm full of comfort rather than complaints. Verse 5 speaks of God preparing a feast for us in the presence of our enemies.

Can you trust God enough today to sit and feast and celebrate inside while fear thunders and crashes its doom down outside?

> *He will cover you with his feathers,*
> *and under his wings you will find refuge;*
> *his faithfulness will be your shield and rampart.*
> Psalm 91: 4 (NIV)

Sit in your heavenly Father's presence today and just let Him speak truth into your heart. Think on all of the goodness you can claim as a daughter of the Most High God. Claim it, Mama! Praise Him today for His rest, His peace, His restoration, His guidance, His presence, His provision, His goodness and His love.

He sees you and your family and He knows your heart. Let Him comfort you like only He can today.

Discipling Point:

The next time you get the mail, grab all that junk mail and give it to your kiddos to rip up and throw around. I know, messy right? It should get stuck in their hair, on their clothes, etc. But then tell them they must make a tent (or crawl into one if they have one), and toss the pieces of junk mail at the tent while they safely hide inside. Speak to them about how God loves us and is here to provide a peace-filled refuge for us, regardless of what is going on in our lives. He will shelter us through the storms (Psalm 91:4-7).

I am SEEN when I:

God's Whispers:

Prayer

God, I'm tired. I'm tired of feeling tired. Please gather me in close through this season. Hold me up, because I can't stand up through it alone. Thank you that I have access to your supernatural strength. You are my steady rock when I am weary. Please help me to find moments of rest today so I can best love on those around me.
Amen.

My Prayers:

He refreshes my soul. He guides me along the right paths for his name's sake.

Psalm 23:3 (NIV)

Day 15

Pray for wisdom and read: **Isaiah 40:1-31; Psalm 28**

_____

_____

Isaiah 40:11

Be a Shepherd, Mama

In Isaiah 40:11 we see that our Shepherd God will gather and gently lead His people at Christ's second coming. And as I strive to model our Shepherd to care for my little lambs, I have looked more closely at the job of a shepherd.

- They often work in isolated areas by themselves.
- They work around the clock, keeping an eye on their flock 24/7.
- They must look out for dangerous predators as well as poisonous plants that the animals might try to eat.
- They are outnumbered by sheep.

Are you seeing any correlations to motherhood? I sure am. Even in a world of online connectivity, motherhood can feel lonely some days. There are no vacation days or even weekends in motherhood. After loving and training and playing and kissing boo-boo's and cleaning up spills and feeding and bathing and cuddling and feeding and cleaning…we wake up throughout the night to cuddle and clean sheets and dry tears even as our own tears flow.

So how do we walk through this pasture of motherhood? We look up, sweet Mama. We learn from our Shepherd God how to have and show grace and love. We ask for wisdom to train and lead…and we plead with Him for copious amounts of patience and endurance.

I look to David's words in the Psalms when I am feeling like a lone shepherd. David spent many years in the quiet of the fields, listening for God's voice and allowing God to shape his heart for GREAT things to come. I pray for God to keep me from filling my days up with busyness through this pasturing season of motherhood, realizing He is teaching me to lean in, listen, take courage in and have a relationship with Him. I trust He is preparing me for GREAT things— and I pray that as you are in your pasturing years of motherhood, that you know He is doing the same for you.

Allow your heavenly Father to gently lead and guide you in your mothering today. Whisper prayers to Him when you feel lost. He will help you find your way.

Discipling Point:

Don't shy away from speaking SOME of your prayers aloud, Mama. As I go through my days, there are moments that are so crazy, I find myself just raising my hands and saying, "Jesus, be near. God, help me to be kind, help me to have extra patience, help me to love better. Amen." And my kids hear me. And you know what? I'm teaching and training them to be REAL emotionally-healthy parents one day. Model where your eyes gaze when life feels crazy, so they will know where to look when they experience challenging days.

I am SEEN when I:

-
-
-
-
-

God's Whispers:

Prayer

God, thank you so much for Shepherding me daily through this pasture of motherhood. Remind me when I am overwhelmed that my little sheep are YOUR little sheep. Keep me looking up for YOUR wisdom, direction and protection. Show me how to best guide my children today and always. Amen.

My Prayers:

He will gently lead the mother sheep with their young.

Isaiah 40:11b (NLT)

Day 16

Pray for wisdom and read: **2 Kings 6:1-23**

2 Kings 6:12

God Knows. Find Comfort in That.

I was reading through 1 and 2 Kings recently and was captivated by the story of the prophets Elijah and Elisha. I was moved when they "knew" things that humans alone cannot know. In 2 Kings chapter 6, Elisha knows what the king of Aram is planning over and over. Verse 12 says that Elisha tells the king of Israel the very words that the king of Aram speaks in his bedroom.

There is so much to take from this passage, but I pray you find comfort in knowing that God KNOWS everything. EVERYTHING. And then some.

As in, God knows things we can't even know we don't know! If God supplies the kind of supernatural knowledge to these prophets that sets us in awe, how much MORE must our God know? These are His prophets, but they are still human with finite power. God's power is infinite.

I pray that as you look at your days ahead and maybe are feeling a bit weary about what is to come (job insecurity, health issues, loss, parenting challenges, education choices for your children, daily life interruptions)…that you remember whose daughter you are.

You are the daughter of a God who knows everything that is to come already, and He is holding you in His hand, sweet one! He wants what is best for you (Jer. 29:11).

Look forward with CONFIDENCE, knowing that HE KNOWS EVERYTHING. Press into Him when you begin to feel unsteady so that He can strengthen you and remind you that He's got it. Leave your Bible open on the counter, write verses that encourage you on your mirror or kitchen window with washable markers, turn on worship music, and pray for strength. He loves you so much, Mama! Let the God of the Universe hold you rock steady through this world.

 Discipling Point:

Buy a bag of dum-dum suckers and pull out all of the mystery flavors. Hold the sucker bouquet in your hand and have your kids choose one. If they are like my littlest ones, they might ask what flavor they are. Tell them it's a surprise, but promise they will taste sweet. Talk to them about how God doesn't reveal all of His plans for us, but that He promises they will be good for us. This is a wonderful opportunity to plant a seed of faith, Mama! Look for other moments in your mothering that God prompts you to speak His truths into your sweet ones' hearts.

I am SEEN when I:

-
-
-
-
-

God's Whispers:

Prayer

God, I don't know what lies ahead and am so uncertain about so much, but I trust you. I find comfort knowing that YOU know what is to come even when I do not. Will you please remind me of your love for me and my family today? We need you as we step forward into what to us is unknown. Place our feet on your eternal firm ground, rather than the finite ground of this world. We know you have good in store for us.
Amen.

My Prayers:

"None of us, my lord the king," said one of his officers, "but Elisha, the prophet who is in Israel, tells the king of Israel the very words you speak in your bedroom."

2 Kings 6:12 (NIV)

Day 17

Pray for wisdom and read: **2 Timothy 1:1-18**

2 Timothy 1:7

Make Me Steady in the Face of Fear

My five-year-old said something profound the other evening while talking with me and making up a game. He was talking about feeling fearful of heights. I mentioned to him that when he was two years old, he flew across the country in a plane. His reply? "When you're young you don't understand as much so you're not scared. When you're older, you fear more." Truth from the mouth of babes.

I'm sure your kids have said similar truths that stopped you in your tracks. God teaches us all the time as mamas, right? I loved his comment because it made me reflect on why it is so challenging as an adult to "have faith." Fear definitely plays a role in our ability to believe in something.

- Fear that while believing in something better, our circumstance will not get better, in fact it might even get

worse.
- Fear that God's plan might not line up with ours—and might not feel comfortable to us.
- Fear that we really don't have as much control in this world as we like to think we have.

My three-year-old daughter lives with no fear these days. I find her on counters, on top of the dryer, running around on top of the dining room table, up in the linen closet, upside down on the couch, climbing ladders…she is a new level of fearless in our house, and when I approach her in her explorations of danger limits, she always states very confidently, "God made me steady, Mom."

We have never told her this, but it is her daily mantra. It's become a family phrase. And as I read in 2 Timothy, I long to have her same fierce steadiness in the way I live, realizing God's spirit of power, love and self-control in my life. I pray for the same steadiness for you as you approach new daily challenges. He SEES you and is WITH you, sweet one!

Discipling Point:

The next time you are going for a walk and your child decides to walk along the curb or on top of a wall and you're holding his or her hand, mention how God has made him or her steady. Plant those words into your little one's heart today that they might float to mind later in life when he or she is feeling shaky.

I am SEEN when I:

God's Whispers:

Prayer

God, make me steady in my faith and belief in you. Thank you for placing your Spirit of power, love and self-control in me. Keep reminding me that you see me and that you love me and that you are with me for eternity. I long to live so steady in you that whatever the world throws my way, I will still stand and live for you. Amen.

My Prayers:

For God gave us a spirit not of fear but of power and love and self-control.
2 Timothy 1:7 (ESV)

Day 18

Pray for wisdom and read: **Psalm 34**

Psalm 34:18-19

Hope: It's Yours for the Taking!

There was a time in my life when I was so broken I wasn't sure I would wake up the next day. While seeking help and healing, someone wise once told me it was okay to ride the coat-tails of someone in my life who believed in me until I could believe in me.

If you don't have that someone in your life, let me be that someone and tell you that if you are still breathing breath here on this earth, then **God has a plan for your life**!

If you believe that Jesus Christ is God's Son and came to this earth in the flesh to save us from our sins, and have asked Him into your heart, then you are a Believer. That comes with some benefits, my dear one.

- God CHOSE YOU. You are chosen.

- You are wanted.
- You are loved.
- You are forgiven.

Bathe your mind in His Word, friend. There are so many verses of hope you can claim as a Believer. I can point you to a few, but don't stop here. Open up God's living Word and let Him speak to Your heart as only He can do. He SEES you and longs to spend time with you.

Verses of Hope:

> *Let us hold unswervingly to the hope we profess,*
> *for he who promised is faithful.*
> Hebrews 10:23 (NIV)

> *The moon will shine like the sun and the sunlight will be seven times brighter, like the light of seven full days, when the Lord binds up the bruises of his people and heals the wounds he inflicted.*
> Isaiah 30:26 (NIV)

 *Discipling Point:*

Write out one of the verses that moves your heart to believe in God's plan for your life and tape it to your bathroom mirror. Read it while you brush your teeth. Read it when you put away towels. Read it when your toddler makes fluffy cloud pillows out of that mega-sized new toilet paper roll. And when your children ask you what it says, read it to them and tell them that God has plans for their lives that you can't even imagine. Build up those little BIG hearts today, Mama. Be their "I believe in you" person.

I am SEEN when I:

God's Whispers:

Prayer

God, thank you so much for graciously choosing me. For loving me. For wanting me. I am so humbled to know you. When I am feeling hopeless, pull me into your living Word and into your arms. Remind me that you have a plan for my life. Please bring people into my life that remind me of my worth in you as well. Amen.

My Prayers:

The LORD is near to the brokenhearted and saves those who are crushed in spirit. Many are the afflictions of the righteous, but the LORD delivers him out of them all.

Psalm 34:18-19 (NASB)

Day 19

Pray for wisdom and read: **Proverbs 16:1-33; Philippians 4:6-7; Isaiah 26:3**

Proverbs 16:32

Processing

Did you know that our minds are not made to process endless information? That we are not made to be computers for a reason? That we need to allow for processing of our emotions for every morsel of information that we choose to input into our brains?

Information scientists have quantified that humans now process 34 Gigs of information a day. If we were made as computers strictly to process information, that's not a big deal. Computers don't have the emotional energy algorithm computed into them. We humans do.

If you are a mother, you have been given the precious role of emotional processor for your children. One of your roles as a mother is to help your kids talk through what they have experienced in their day. If you are married, then you have an additional human to play this role for. And YOU need someone to process through your day with. Be careful not to intake more information than you can healthfully process on a daily basis. Now, can you control everything that happens to you? Absolutely NOT. But in our current culture of information overload, we have way more choice in this than we want to admit.

Do we really need to read endless news stories or other people's social life feeds on a daily basis?

Leave room today for the precious hearts that God has physically placed before you. By limiting your own information overload, you will be saving up enough emotional output to give to your cherished ones in front of you. SEE your little ones and their gorgeous eyes, Mama. They need you to SEE them.

Discipling Point:

Limit your information intake today a bit more than you usually do. See if it gives you more emotional energy to connect with your little ones before you. Focus on eye contact with them and listening to their hearts. They contain worlds.

I am SEEN when I:

God's Whispers:

Prayer

God, thank you for the gift of my mind and my emotions. Thank you that I am not a mere robot, programmed to do your will. Father, I long to please your heart. Please help me to manage my life, mind and spirit by limiting my intake of those things that I do not need to focus on so that I have the energy and focus to best love you and those around me well.
Amen.

My Prayers:

He who is slow to anger is better than the mighty, And he who rules his spirit, than he who captures a city.

Proverbs 16:32 (NASB)

Day 20

Pray for wisdom and read: **Acts 1:1-11**

_____

_____

Acts 1:7

More Than We Can Conceive

I love verses 4-8 of today's reading in Acts. Jesus hints at a promise from God that is about to happen (the power of the Holy Spirit coming upon them following Jesus' ascension into heaven). The disciples ask if God's kingdom is about to be restored to Israel. Jesus reminds them in verse 7 that only God knows these things.

The disciples can't even fathom the Holy Spirit, let alone what it means to be given the Spirit's POWER.

Their finite minds could not conceive of what was coming because God is always BIGGER. His ways cannot be simplified to human understanding.

My husband and I once jumped into a car with $200 to our names and tent-camped our way to new jobs and a new locale. It was one of the wildest years of our lives, and yet the most affirming in our faith in God. That year sealed forever on our hearts that a life lived for Christ means a life of adventure!

After that year, we dreamed of being parents. We spent years on our knees, pleading for a positive pregnancy test. But as we spent more time in His presence waiting, God opened our eyes to His beautiful plans for beginning our family through adoption. He redeemed what was broken and crafted a beautiful family in His hands. We learned that He is the author of families, and continue to marvel at His plans as we watch our four precious little ones grow and love and learn.

Our minds, our five-year and ten-year plans? They are limited, friends. **Don't dethrone His authority in your lives.** When you make plans, realize they are limited, and welcome His radical changes to them, knowing He has your best interest at heart—YOUR heart.

Lean into God through prayer and His Word. Listen for His voice and His direction for your lives. He wants your heart, and He knows more than you can possibly dream up. Don't miss out on God's plans. Adventuring through life with Him in the lead will always leave you with the best stories to tell!

Discipling Point:

The next time your child asks you the timing of something you just can't give a definite answer for, comfort them by adding that God knows. You might not know when their first tooth will come out or when they will meet their future spouse, but God does know and will reveal it in His most perfect timing. Remind your child that if you knew how everything was going to play out, there would be no surprises in our lives. Remind them of their birthday surprises as an analogy.

I am SEEN when I:

-
-
-
-
-

God's Whispers:

Prayer

God, thank you so much that I do NOT know everything. It takes the pressure off of my human need for control. When I let you work, knowing you love me and want what is best for me, I can more readily accept what you place before me. You truly lead us into more than we could ever dream up or imagine. I am so humbled and honored to be your daughter.
Amen.

My Prayers:

He said to them, 'It is not for you to know the times or dates the Father has set by his own authority.'

Acts 1:7 (NIV)

Day 21

Pray for wisdom and read: **Mark 14:1-42; Jonah 1:17; Psalm 139:15-16**

Psalm 139:15-16

God Knows What is Coming Today

I am always in awe of God's foreknowledge and preparation. Verses 13-16 and 30 of today's reading in Mark are an amazing example of this. I was reading in Psalm 139:15-16 recently and love the parallel thought.

Do you ever stop to think of how God is preparing a way for you? And not just in terms of your overall life, but TODAY.

When I live aware of my eternal place, I do things like pause and pray with the checkout lady who shares her heart with me, and I stop to pull out a granola bar from my purse to give to the houseless man sitting on the curb. When I am NOT focused on God's ordination of my life's days, I become so self-focused that I am certain I miss countless eternally important encounters.

Likewise, when I live aware that God has plans for my life, I walk confidently into situations that feel scary and yet are important for me to grow and love others better. I find God's Spirit giving me confidence to not only act but also speak love and His Truth into those around me.

As you read this, God KNOWS what is to come, and He will walk with you through it. Walk confidently with your Savior today, sweet Mama. Watch for God-ordained meetings and treat them as such.

As C.S. Lewis says in "The Weight of Glory", "There are no ordinary people. You have never talked to a mere mortal. Nations, cultures, arts, civilizations—these are mortal, and their life is to ours as the life of a gnat. But it is immortals whom we joke with, work with, marry, snub and exploit—immortal horrors or everlasting splendors."

Your interactions matter today. Live them with this eternal awareness.

Discipling Point:

The next time your child feels anxious about an upcoming event, share Psalm 139:15-16 with him or her. Remind your child that God has a plan for his/her life and that he/she can walk forward in confidence, knowing God goes with him/her into whatever looms scary before him/her.

I am SEEN when I:

-
-
-
-
-

God's Whispers:

Prayer

God, I am humbled as I read your Word and see your foreknowledge at work. I trust that you know what is coming in my life today, and I lean into my belief in Jeremiah 29:10—that you have planned GOOD for me. Thank you for preparing my heart every day to accept whatever you lay before me.
Amen.

My Prayers:

My frame was not hidden from you when I was made in the secret place, when I was woven together in the depths of the earth. Your eyes saw my unformed body; all the days ordained for me were written in your book before one of them came to be.

Psalm 139:15-16 (NIV)

Day 22

Pray for wisdom and read: **2 Timothy 2**

2 Timothy 2:13

He Remains Faithful

As I read through today's verses, and particularly verses 11-13, I'm encouraged, convicted, and reassured.

There is so much HOPE in knowing Christ! I often find myself just praising God for the absolute gift it is to KNOW Him. Daily, I am aware that because I KNOW Jesus, everything changes.

My worldview changes. My focus shifts from pleasing myself to pleasing God. My parenting tactics change—it's no longer about me being right and lording my power over my child—or the opposite, being my child's spoiling parent out to win over their heart as the coolest mom around.

Because I know Jesus, I realize there are eternal stakes in my choices to choose love and mercy and grace as I raise and daily sacrifice my wants to help shape and support my little ones' just-forming, tender hearts.

Because I know Jesus, I respond differently to my colleague's when they make mistakes, because I've received grace, I can give grace.

Because I know Jesus, I can forgive myself and ask for forgiveness when I make a mistake.

Because I know Jesus, I can ignore unkind comments and judgments from people because I know that I am forgiven and justified, I am beautifully crafted, and God has incredible plans for my life—plans to prosper me and not to harm me, plans to give me a hope and a future (Jer. 29:11).

Because I know Jesus, I am invited to weep at His feet, praise Him when my heart feels song, and seek His supernatural, all-knowing wisdom.

Every. Moment. To know Him is to realize that even if I doubt Him, He cannot doubt Himself. God isn't going anywhere, sweet one. When you choose to root yourself to Him, you will stand firm.

 *Discipling Point:*

Live in the peace, joy and hope of the Lord today, Mama! The climate you create in your home matters. One of my children tends to lean towards the negative side of life, and one day in exasperation, he quipped, "How can you be so joyful all the time, Mom?" I told him because I have the hope of Jesus and all that comes with that (see above). I saw his heart slowly soak this in. Speak truth to your littles' hearts. Their questions will get bigger as they grow. Be ready to point up, Mama keeping your relationship with Jesus strong.

I am SEEN when I:

God's Whispers:

Prayer

God, it is such an honor to know you, to be chosen by you, to be loved by you, to be justified by you. I rest in this today and praise you for being my God. I love you and give you my days.
Amen.

My Prayers:

If we are faithless, he remains faithful, for he cannot disown himself.
2 Timothy 2:13 (NIV)

Day 23

Pray for wisdom and read: **Ezra 4-6**

_____
_____

Ezra 4:4-5

Discouragement Will Come

I have been studying the history of Israel, and after God's people were punished and sent to Babylon for 70 years, God called them back to Jerusalem to rebuild His temple and the city. Suddenly, the following verse I have always loved took on a whole new light as I realized the weight of God's promise to restore His people tucked within its words:

> "For I know the plans I have for you," declares the Lord, "plans to prosper you and not to harm you, plans to give you hope and a future. Then you will call on me and come and pray to me, and I will listen to you. You will seek me and find me when you seek me with all your heart. I will be found by you," declares the Lord, "and will bring you back from captivity."
> Jeremiah 29:11-13a

After God's people returned to Jerusalem and began rebuilding the Temple of God, they were met with discouragement from the people of the land.

Mamas, if you are choosing to pour God's light, love and truth into your home and build up holy ground to grow and train your kids in, guess what? You are laying foundations for God's kingdom that Satan cannot bear to see. Just like God's people rebuilding Jerusalem, you are going to face discouragement, fear and frustrated plans.

AND YET! Remember that God is watching over you, and as you commit your life to Him, His hand will be upon you!

But the eye of their God was watching over the elders of the Jews, and they were not stopped…
Ezra 5:5 (NIV)

God will move hearts just like He moved King Darius to continue to build and restore His kingdom. Pray for God to move hearts and surround you with people to support and love you as you determine to raise your kids in a home built on God's Word.

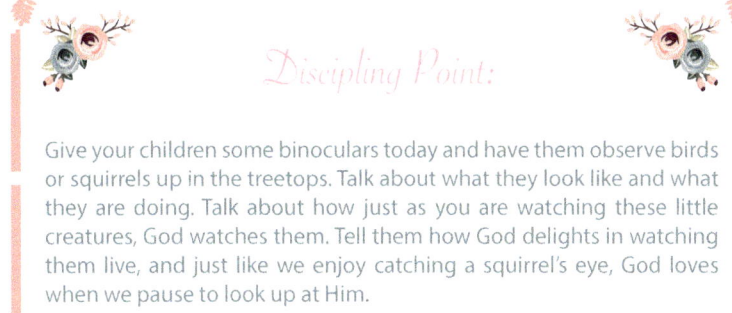

Discipling Point:

Give your children some binoculars today and have them observe birds or squirrels up in the treetops. Talk about what they look like and what they are doing. Talk about how just as you are watching these little creatures, God watches them. Tell them how God delights in watching them live, and just like we enjoy catching a squirrel's eye, God loves when we pause to look up at Him.

I am SEEN when I:

God's Whispers:

Prayer

God, thank you for the reminder today that your eye is watching me and that you SEE me. As I face discouragement in _____, please send me reminders of your promises for goodness in my life as I daily pursue you and determine to point my family's hearts up to you. I love you. Amen.

My Prayers:

Then the peoples around them set out to discourage the people of Judah and make them afraid to go on building. They bribed officials to work against them and frustrate their plans...

Ezra 4:4-5 (NIV)

Day 24

Pray for wisdom and read: **James 1:1-12; 1 Peter 1:1-7; Romans 5:1-5**

Romans 5:3-5

Delight in Suffering

The word "glory" defined as a verb is: to take great pride or pleasure in. Some synonyms listed are: revel in, rejoice in, delight in, relish, savor, boast about, bask in.

God wants us to delight and bask in the GOODNESS of suffering. What?! This is the opposite of complaining or victimizing ourselves.

Certain needs in our home have left me depleted many days. Before understanding God's work in reshaping my selfish human heart through the challenges, I would find myself ticking off a list of all the struggles as my husband returned home from work. Just what he needed to hear after a long day out in the world, right?

God has reshaped my heart in this area over the years, and I now realize that struggle keeps me on my knees. It gives me endurance, empathy and a deeper faith and understanding of unconditional love. Do I still process the hard with my husband and closest friends? Absolutely. But I do so with an acceptance that we all have our "hard" places in life to grow, rather than a hopeless woe-is-me heart.

Be joy-filled, sweet sisters when you are struggling: struggling with anxiety, struggling with illness, struggling through grief, struggling with infertility, struggling with loneliness, struggling with fear, struggling with challenging attitudes and relationships in or outside your home, struggling with finances, struggling to find sleep, struggling with your body image, struggling with_____.

Think about it this way: God loves you so much that He is allowing you to stretch and grow in a beautiful way—in character and in faith. Keep your eyes up, sweet one. God is WITH you and He SEES you. Right. Where. You. Are. He is doing a good work in and through you. Choose to trust Him through the hard today, and point to Him when someone asks you how you're making it through. He loves you so much!

Discipling Point:

The next time your child's room needs cleaning, go and help your child for a bit and find a moment to work in how it isn't exactly fun to clean up, but the end result sure feels good. Talk about how you have been learning that God allows suffering to produce perseverance, character and hope. And if there is a struggle more significantly looming before your child than a clean room today, use your knowledge of God's Word to speak hope into that hurting part of your sweet one's life.

I am SEEN when I:

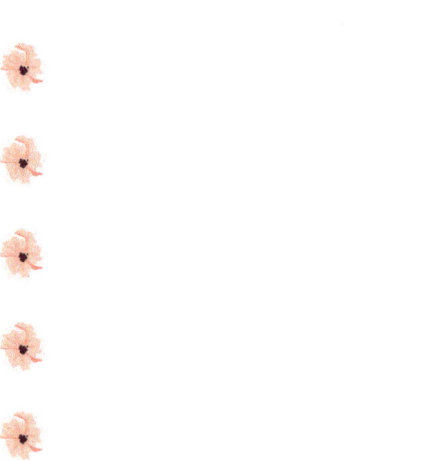

God's Whispers:

Prayer

God, check my heart in how I am perceiving…and SHARING about my suffering. May my tone be one of delight rather than woeful misery. God, your work on my heart is such a beautiful blessing! Amen.

My Prayers:

Not only so, but we also glory in our sufferings, because we know that suffering produces perseverance; perseverance, character; and character, hope. And hope does not put us to shame, because God's love has been poured out into our hearts through the Holy Spirit, who has been given to us.

Romans 5:3-5

Day 25

Pray for wisdom and read: **2 Corinthians 4; Proverbs 17:22**

---

2 Corinthians 4:16-18

Proverbs 17:22

It's About Your Heart Attitude

As you're singing your daughter her favorite good-night song request, are you singing it while thinking about the laundry in the dryer or the dishes on the counter? Or are you fully PRESENT in the moment and realizing the magnitude of the moment you will look back on one day?

Will you look back and feel content knowing you fully LIVED and LOVED your sweet little ones with everything you had to give them while they were still stationed under the same roof as you?

I have had moments where I realized I was just going through the motions. An extra-full day can lead to me pushing through the bedtime routine and my 5-year-old saying, "Mom, you read that book really fast." Oops. Or how about those homeschool days in the frosty depths of February when dreary-no-sun-days make me unable to produce an extra ounce of fun in our daily routine?

What I'm learning is that if I can recognize a trend in such moments, I can find ways to adjust my heart attitude. I pause and pray for an eternal perspective, and God gives it to me.

Take a look at your precious baby (or teenager or adult child!) before you. Yes, even that 95-pound man-baby before your eyes (mamas with fast-growing boys, you get me, right?), and soak him in!!! He is yours! He is to be treasured! He is learning how to love HIS babies by the way you stay present and love him!

Remember today that 18 birthdays under your roof fly by…and while we are parents forever, these years together every day truly are precious and fleeting. Sing that song one more time. Linger before kissing your babe good-night. Think back on the first time you held your sweet one. Take that extra moment to whisper an extra prayer over the precious gift of life God has entrusted you to love.

Live in a way that you will never look back and regret. Those dishes? They will get done at some point. That laundry? As a mother of four, I have accepted it will never get done. But it will be tamed in time. For now, I'm going to go kiss my deeply-breathing for-once-all-sleep-dreaming precious pieces of my heart.

 *Discipling Point:*

The next time your little one is having a mumbly, grumbly kind of day, remind him or her that this day only comes one time. They can choose to live this once-in-a-lifetime day with a thankful heart or a grumbly heart, but they will not get it back for a redo. Give them time to process and see what they decide. Regardless, remember that you are the best model for your children, and that you are not called to take on your children's emotions. If a child is particularly gloomy, pray for extra strength to remain encouraging, calm, gracious and loving so your overall family climate remains steady.

I am SEEN when I:

God's Whispers:

Prayer

God, thank you so much for the honor of being entrusted with these precious children. Help me to stay present today as I love them, realizing our days are fleeting. Thank you so much for making me a mama. Thank you so much for seeing me. Help me to make sure my children feel SEEN today as well.
Amen.

My Prayers:

Therefore we do not lose heart. Though outwardly we are wasting away, yet inwardly we are being renewed day by day. For our light and momentary troubles are achieving for us an eternal glory that far outweighs them all. So we fix our eyes not on what is seen, but what is unseen, since what is seen is temporary, but what is unseen is eternal.
2 Corinthians 4:16-18 (NIV)

A cheerful heart is good medicine, but a crushed spirit dries up the bones.
Proverbs 17:22 (NIV)

Day 26

Pray for wisdom and read: **1 Peter 4**

1 Peter 4:8-11

In Whose Strength Do You Serve?

1 Peter 4 talks about how we are to use our God-given gifts to serve others. 1 Peter 4:11 goes on to say that we are to lean into the origin of our gifts. We aren't merely instructed to serve others if that is our gifting, but we are to serve others WITH THE STRENGTH THAT GOD PROVIDES.

The reason why this is so important is because when we allow God to work through us, not only do we serve at our full capacity, but GOD IS PRAISED and glorified for the work we are doing BY HIS STRENGTH. The key here is that WE are removed from the credit. Our service is not done by our strength, but by God's strength in us.

May our motivation be that of serving by God's strength, and then pointing to HIM when people ask us how we do it. When I take four kids under the age of 7 to two different baseball practices and people ask how I do it, I know it is because of God's strength as I whisper prayers for help… and thus, I must point up to Him and give credit where it is due. When people ask how I work and homeschool my kids and spend time training them and loving them all day, I must give credit where it is due. By pointing up to God and praising Him for what He is doing through you, you will keep your perspective in check so you don't become overwhelmed, and you will also encourage those around you to realize their full capacity when they do the same.

The next time I want to complain or find myself overwhelmed, I'm keeping this verse nearby so I can remember by whose strength I serve. Then I'm going to thank Him, and step forward.

Discipling Point:

Take a moment today to highlight some of the gifts God has given your kids. Talk to them about how they can step forward confidently to use their gifts to serve others, knowing God is the source of these gifts. And give them an example to follow the next time someone compliments something you do well by being quick to give glory where it's due. This world screams for us to prove our worth, sweet mamas. Remember that you have been deemed worthy already—worthy enough for the beloved Son of the God most High to die for your mistakes. Don't take the glory—willingly give it to the source of Who makes us "good." Your humble heart and response will be noticed by your children, and remember they can only emulate what they see. Be a part of the good you long for their hearts to soak in and spill out.

I am SEEN when I:

God's Whispers:

Prayer

God, thank you so much for creating me just as you have. Give me courage today to use my spiritual giftings to love those around me. I trust you to supply the strength and motivation I need to best love those around me, and I give you the glory for the work you will do as I choose obedience to your calling in my life.
Amen.

My Prayers:

Above all, love each other deeply, because love covers over a multitude of sins. Offer hospitality to one another without grumbling. Each of you should use whatever gift you have received to serve others, as faithful stewards of God's grace in its various forms. If anyone speaks, they should do so as one who speaks the very words of God. If anyone serves, they should do so with the strength God provides, so that in all things God may be praised through Jesus Christ. To him be the glory and the power for ever and ever. Amen.

1 Peter 4:8-11 (NIV)

Day 27

Pray for wisdom and read: **Deuteronomy 6:1-9; 11:18-25**

Deuteronomy 6:7 (NASB)

Bookend Your Day with the Word

I climbed into bed tonight and I let out a deep breath. It had been a long bedtime routine, and yet I felt satisfied. My youngest ones had requested nearly every story in their bible (seriously, I read 104 pages). And after reading a popular children's chapter book to my oldest two, they requested a "happy Bible story" afterward to have fresh on their minds and hearts before going to sleep.

Thinking of our morning Bible reading at breakfast, I realized that my kids' day had been sandwiched between God's Word. What a blessing! These are the hidden places where your extra intentional moments to read God's Word (or your choice to listen and obey the Spirit's promptings through your children's hearts to read His Word) matter, Mama.

Bedtime routines can feel exhausting. Before we started our routine tonight, I hugged my husband and whispered, "I don't want to start bedtime…"

The endless extra cups of water, extra trips to the potty, extra need to change pajamas, extra prayers, extra stories, extra…requires a whole lot of EXTRA patience. BUT, when we choose extra patience and love and choose to be present and listen to the Spirit's promptings, we can fall asleep with a special satisfied joy in our hearts, realizing God is using us in our children's faith stories.

What an honor and privilege it is to be the one to read Psalms of hope to my boys that will one day be men—that they will have their Mom's voice speaking God's truth into their memories. When I realize the eternal repercussions of choosing to be present and reading just a little more of His Word when I feel beyond spent for the day, I find the energy for it. I pray you do as well.

 Discipling Point:

Do your kiddos have a Bible next to their bed? If not, make a way to get one there. One of my boys struggled to read, but he poured over *The Action Bible* on his own. And I keep a devotional and Bible in a cabinet I can reach from our breakfast table. Make preparations to sandwich your sweet ones' days in God's Word. And don't sweat a missed day. God doesn't want perfection. He wants your hearts.

I am SEEN when I:

-
-
-
-
-

God's Whispers:

Prayer

God, please give me supernatural energy and awareness today of the eternal impact my faith walk in You has on my children. Move me to speak more of Your eternal truths and love for my sweet ones today. Bookend our days in Your Word. Make me bold in my declarations of Your plans for my husband, my children and those around me. You. Have. Plans. I love you. Amen.

My Prayers:

You shall teach them diligently to your sons and shall talk of them when you sit in your house and when you walk by the way and when you lie down and when you rise up.

Deuteronomy 6:7 (NASB)

Day 28

Pray for wisdom and read: **1 Corinthians 6**

---

1 Corinthians 6:11

Ignore that Voice of Judgment, Sweet Mama!

You know the voice. It seems to grow louder the more tired or more defeated you feel. The one that says you're not doing enough. You're not taking your kids enough places. You're not reading to your kids enough. You're not providing enough hands-on-homemade-glitter-playdough experiences with your kids. You yell too much. You don't hug them enough. You didn't say the right thing to comfort them. Well, guess what?

Mamas are imperfect human beings. All of us humans are. Now read that verse up at the top of the page again, sweet one. Now read it *again* and CLAIM IT over your life and your family. You do NOT have to live up to any outside voice that tells you that you are not enough. You know how much you are striving everyday to be "enough" of every title you've been given: enough of a mom, enough of a wife, enough of a friend, enough of a daughter, enough of a sister, enough of co-worker, enough of a ___.

Whatever your striving is, take a deeeeeep breath and remember that through Jesus, you are ENOUGH. By accepting Jesus as your Lord and Savior and asking Him into your heart, you are enough. He is the judge and you are enough. So ignore the judgmental voices from the world. Let them go right on judging you, because they don't matter.

Daily spend time with your Savior in prayer and in His living Word, and walk out the life He directs you to. Don't let false outside judgmental voices distract you from the work God is calling you to today.

God SEES you and all that you are doing and all the ways you are choosing love every day. You are free to live, Mama!

Discipling Point:

When your children come to you feeling left out of a group or feeling like they are not good enough, remind them of the truths you have just read—that they are fully justified and loved by God and by you. Remind them not to listen to the world's judgment. If they are reading, write out 1 Corinthians 6:11 on a notecard and place it on their dresser with a note of love and acceptance from you, Mama. And if they are younger, take them into the bathroom for "mirror time." Hold them up on the counter and have them repeat affirmations to themself. Examples: I am loved. I am chosen. God has amazing plans for me. I am beautiful. I am smart. I give the best hugs.

I am SEEN when I:

-
-
-
-
-

God's Whispers:

Prayer

Thank you, God, for freeing me to live a full life free of other people's judgment. Thank you for justifying me through my acceptance of your Son Jesus Christ in my heart. Remind me of this when I begin to allow Satan's lies to seep into my thoughts. I am justified. I am free to live life to the full! I praise you for that! Amen.

My Prayers:

But you were washed, you were sanctified, you were justified in the name of the Lord Jesus Christ and by the Spirit of our God.

1 Corinthians 6:11 (NIV)

Day 29

Pray for wisdom and read: **2 Corinthians 12**

2 Corinthians 12:9

A Piece of Cake

Crying. Whining. Endless attitude. It was a Sunday afternoon and my son was trying my patience. I had offered numerous suggestions for entertainment, hugs, etc. to no avail. Nothing was working and he just kept whimpering around the house. Our three other children were happily occupied. Feeling out of options, I was about to send this child to his room for fifteen minutes, more to give myself a break from his negative attitude than anything.

But then, God whispered, "Kendra, do the opposite." "You mean, show him even more grace? What more can I do?" I whined in my mind. And then I remembered that there was one piece of birthday cake left in the house.

So as my son sat at the kitchen table, tears still wetting his eyes, I took a deep breath in and exhaled out, smiling at him. I walked over to the cupboard and carefully pulled out two flowered plates and mugs. I went to the dining room and brought back the glass cake stand holding the final piece of cake. I carefully sliced it down the middle, placing a piece on each plate with a fork, filled the mugs with milk, and carried them over to the table.

As I placed the cake in front of my son, his lip quivered and he wiped his tears with the back of his hand. Not much was said, but as we shared our cake and milk, his eyes met mine and a tiny smile said this was just what he needed. "Mom, I'm saving the best bite for last. Just like you do." And we both savored the final frosting-laden piece, giggling.

After we carried our plates over to the sink, he gave me a hug and whispered, "Thank you, Mom." That was it. Afterwards, he was back to himself, happily playing the afternoon away. I stood at the kitchen sink swallowing a lump in my throat, praising God for shared cake and for His direction and the presence to hear and obey it.

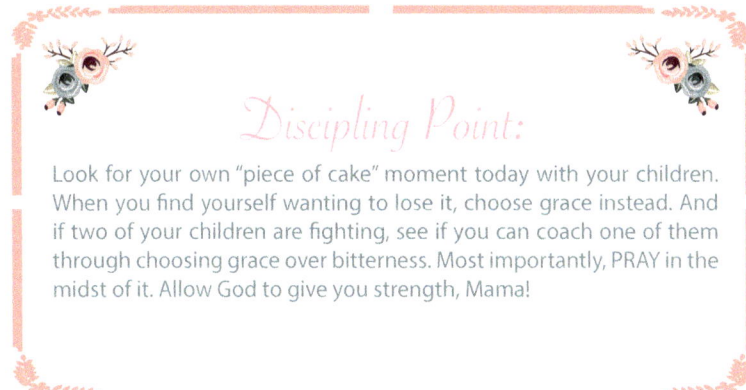

Discipling Point:

Look for your own "piece of cake" moment today with your children. When you find yourself wanting to lose it, choose grace instead. And if two of your children are fighting, see if you can coach one of them through choosing grace over bitterness. Most importantly, PRAY in the midst of it. Allow God to give you strength, Mama!

I am SEEN when I:

God's Whispers:

Prayer

God, I pray today that I will stay present even through the tough parenting moments, that I might hear and obey your promptings that have the power to change my children's days. Thank you for the honor of mothering and loving them.
Amen.

My Prayers:

But he said to me, "My grace is sufficient for you, for my power is made perfect in weakness."
2 Corinthians 12:9 (NIV)

Day 30

Pray for wisdom and read: **Matthew 16:13-28**

Matthew 16:24

Are You Willing to Lose Comfort to be Closer to God?

My son went through a period of time around five years old in which he wanted to sleep next to me at night. He had been sleeping on his own for several years at this point, but the fear of unseen monsters in the night was too real and overwhelming with his gifting of imagination (we tried "monster spray", etc. to no avail). He spent months crawling into bed next to me or pulling me to his bed mid-sleep and then would relax his balled-up fists and anxious body and fall back to sleep once I was near.

At one point during this season, a younger sibling transitioned out of a crib. So I was already splitting my time between my husband and I's bed and the mattress on the floor with my transitioning toddler.

In order to be close to me, my fearful, sweet boy would stumble into the toddler's room with a pillow and curl up next to the mattress and fall back asleep. He so longed to be near me he was willing to sleep on the rug of a hard wooden floor in order to do so (I began leaving several soft sleeping bags along with a snuggly blanket for him next to the mattress).

Parenting has taught me so much about God and myself, and once more such a parenting moment raised the following question:

Do I so long to be with God that I will give up my comfort to be closer to Him? Am I really responding to His Word and His directions I feel Him pressing on my heart in a way that is willing to override my desires for His own?

Discipling Point:

Service and sacrifice are some great ways to talk about what a life layed before Jesus looks like. Open your eyes for age-appropriate service opportunities to bring your children in with you. One thing we have done several times is to take our kids to pick up some groceries and drop them off at a food bank on their birthdays. It refocuses our hearts on the gift of our lives and looks forward into our capacity to live another year of serving and loving others.

I am SEEN when I:

-
-
-
-
-

God's Whispers:

Prayer

God, I long to know you more, and yet my sinful human nature longs for the comforts of this world. Please make my desire to know you stronger than my sinful nature. May I pursue a closer relationship with you and a life fully devoted to following your commands with more passion than I pursue my worldly goals. Forgive me when my sinful nature chooses my comfort over closeness to you. I love you and choose to curl up closer to you today, wherever you lead me.
Amen.

My Prayers:

Then Jesus said to his disciples, "Whoever wants to be my disciple must deny themselves and take up their cross and follow me."

Matthew 16:24 (NIV)

Day 31

Pray for wisdom and read: **1 Kings 17**

_____

_____

1 Kings 17:22

Hold Out for the Miracle

Sometimes the deepest miracles of healing come after living out the deepest trusting faith, and then finding yourself questioning all of it. **If you are in the questioning part, friend, hold out for the miracle.**

The widow in today's reading chooses to believe Elijah and sacrifice all she has for him. She and her son are then provided for, along with Elijah. But, then, her son gets sick and dies.

She questions if Elijah has come, "Just to remind her of her sin and to kill her son."

Ouch. Isn't this often what we do when struggles or tragedy come in life? We question all of our faithful moments and faith-filled living and prayers…and even God. We wonder if we're really holy enough or that maybe our sin isn't really forgiven after all.

But praise God, because this isn't the end of the story! **Elijah's faith begins with questioning God—and ends with him pressing even deeper into his faith and belief in God.**

He believes with every ounce of his mental, emotional, spiritual and physical capacity, even covering the boy with his body.

And God heals.

God breathes new LIFE.

So question, Mama. And then believe and press in. **And watch God breathe new life into that which has stopped breathing in your life.**

 Discipling Point:

Set up a treasure hunt for your children with a promised treat at the end. Write clues to lead them to 4-5 locations, leaving an empty box at the end instead of the promised treat. Their response should be confusion and questions...at which point you ask them if they really trust you. If they say, "yes," then lead them to the real treat as promised. Speak to them about how there will be times in life when they pray to God and ask for an answer, and it might not come in the way or the timing that they expect. BUT! If they faithfully believe and trust in Him, the answer will come.

I am SEEN when I:

God's Whispers:

Prayer

God, I don't understand why _____. I thank you that you are gracious and willing to listen to my questions. Please give me strength to keep believing through my questions. Keep me holding out for your miracles, God. Keep me believing that you will breathe life into the broken and dead places into my life. Thank you, Jesus. Amen.

My Prayers:

The LORD heard the voice of Elijah, and the life of the child returned to him and he revived.

1 Kings 17:22 (NASB)

Day 32

Pray for wisdom and read: **1 Samuel 7**

1 Samuel 7:12

Just Say Yes

God was laying something on my heart recently that I was struggling to obey. Every time I was quiet before my Maker, He brought it to my attention, and every day I seemed to hold on to just a little piece of my control in it.

Isn't this how sin works? Because if we aren't fully obeying God, we are disobeying Him.

Some decry growing older, but I'm going to tell you right now that gaining years in your faith walk only adds up to more fuel for obedience to God. When God asks me to do something and I find myself struggling to fully surrender my will in the matter, I have a history with Him. A history of His faithfulness as I have learned to submit to His will. And so do you!

Just as Samuel took a stone and set it up to remember the

Lord's help for the people of Israel, we can do the same. Think of the times when you have fully obeyed God, and think on the results. This is exactly what I did. I grabbed a pen and paper and scrawled out every moment of faithfulness I could recall. My writing quickly became blurry as tears filtered my sight.

Sweet Mama, God is at work in your life, and when He calls you to something, it might not make sense to anyone else on this earth, but if He is calling you, say yes. In fact, SHOUT YES! Because you are CALLED by the God and creator of human hearts. And keep your faith history list nearby for times when the world is speaking opposite of what God is speaking. He is always faithful.

*Note: Samuel named the stone "Ebenezer", which means "stone of hope." Another family idea is to set up your own Ebenezer stone somewhere in your yard with words you paint on it to remind you of God's faithful work in your family's journey through life. Let it stand as a reminder of His faithfulness in your lives.

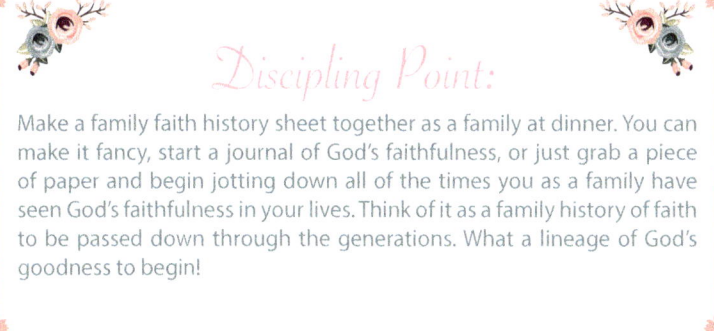

Discipling Point:

Make a family faith history sheet together as a family at dinner. You can make it fancy, start a journal of God's faithfulness, or just grab a piece of paper and begin jotting down all of the times you as a family have seen God's faithfulness in your lives. Think of it as a family history of faith to be passed down through the generations. What a lineage of God's goodness to begin!

I am SEEN when I:

God's Whispers:

Prayer

God, as you call me close to hear your voice, help me to obey despite my sinful selfish nature. Remind me of your faithfulness and help me to say yes to whatever you ask of me today and in the days to come.
I love you so much.
Amen.

My Prayers:

Then Samuel took a stone and set it up between Mispah and Shen. He names it Ebenezer, saying, 'Thus far the Lord has helped us.

1 Samuel 7:12 (NIV)

Day 33

Pray for wisdom and read: **Numbers 14, 2 Kings 10:28-30**

Numbers 14:36-37

With Leadership Comes Responsibility

These verses today remind me that being a child of God doesn't absolve me from punishment. They also reveal something interesting about leadership. God could have simply struck the grumbling people down on the spot, but being the gracious God He is, He allowed them to live out their days in the wilderness. But what about the leaders who went to explore the new land and brought back the grumbling spirit? Those leaders (except for Joshua and Caleb) were struck down and died of a plague.

This example shows me that those in leadership positions are held up to a higher standard. They are required to lead responsibly or they will be dealt with more harshly than those they lead astray.

As a parent you have been given a leadership role, and it is your responsibility not to lead your children away from God or God will deal with you harshly. These verses in Numbers back up verses Mark 9:42 and Matthew 18:6.

> *Whoever causes one of these little ones who believe to stumble, it would be better for him if, with a heavy millstone hung around his neck, he had been cast into the sea.*
>
> Mark 9:42 (NASB)

Realize your influence on every little eye that is watching you today, Mama. Choose to lead their eyes up. Choose to lead their feet into safety. Choose to lead their hands into service. Choose to lead their ears to rich stories of goodness. Choose to lead their hearts toward love. Take your role seriously. You matter. God sees you and the way you are pouring His wisdom and direction into their lives, even when nobody else does. You all will reap eternal blessings for it, and don't forget that your faithful leadership has generational implications.

> *The Lord said to Jehu, "Because you have done well in executing what is right in My eyes, and have done to the house of Ahab according to all that was in My heart, your sons of the fourth generation shall sit on the throne of Israel."*
>
> 2 Kings 10:30 (NASB)

Discipling Point:

Play a game of "Follow-the-Leader" with your kiddos today. Do some extra silly things to make them giggle. Talk with them about leadership and why it is important to be a good leader and also to know what kind of people they are following and spending time with. It's often said that we become most like the five people we spend the most time around. Let these ideas fill your conversations today.

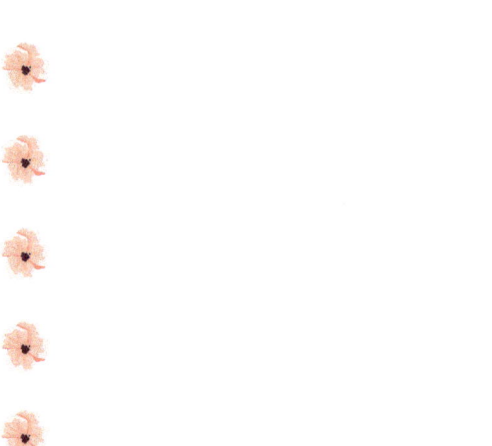

I am SEEN when I:

-
-
-
-
-

God's Whispers:

Prayer

God, I am humbled once again that you would entrust me with being a daily part of shaping the lives of other people—my precious children. Please keep pulling me closer to your heart, that my words, love and actions that I pour out to my children become an extension of you. Please give me wisdom and clarity each day as to how to best love and lead my children. May my everyday life not distract them from the eternal, but rather draw their eyes up to you.
Amen.

My Prayers:

Even those men who brought out the very bad report of the land died by a plague before the LORD.

Numbers 14:37 (NASB)

Day 34

Pray for wisdom and read: **1 Samuel 3**

_____

_____

1 Samuel 3:8b-9

Don't Miss His Voice in the Night

In today's reading, Samuel keeps going to Eli in the temple, thinking that Eli is calling him. And Eli keeps telling him to "go back to bed."

Samuel was really hearing God's voice but thought it was Eli calling for him. Now here is an interesting thought…what if we approach our mommy-middle-of-the-night calls with a holy awareness that God is in this motherhood business and our baby's needs for around-the-clock care?

What if when our kids are waking us in the middle of the night, it's God calling to us as well? As my husband and I have lived through a nearly decade-year-long season of severely sleep-deprived nights…not just a few wake ups here and there—we're talking 6 to 8 wake-ups a night…we have been on our knees with God through them pleading for rest and seeking the purpose of it all. The verses that were pressed on our hearts and comforted us the most during these wakeful hours were:

Let the morning bring me word of your unfailing love, for I have put my trust in you. Show me the way I should go, for to you I entrust my life.
Psalm 143:8 (NIV)

Jesus replied, "You do not realize now what I am doing, but later you will understand."
John 13:7 (NIV)

As we chose to soak in the precious moments holding and comforting our babes, we continue to learn so much: to sit in the quiet and listen for God's voice; to bask in the beauty of a finally sleeping child in our arms; to give more than we ever thought we could; that every child has unique needs and humans are not robots with an all-encompassing magic formula; that maybe everything isn't always about us and that sometimes it's about loving and giving up even more of our innate selfish desires—like that expectant yet elusive sleep our bodies so painfully crave.

 *Discipling Point:*

Call for each of your children at some point today just to hug them and whisper, "I love you," in their ear. Make sure that your calls to them are not just to give them direction or correction, but that you also call them just to remind you of their love for them. Mama, you are modeling a loving parent-child relationship that will affect their view of their Father in heaven/child relationship. Just as they will grow to expect loving words from you, they will learn to look to Jesus for loving words as well.

I am SEEN when I:

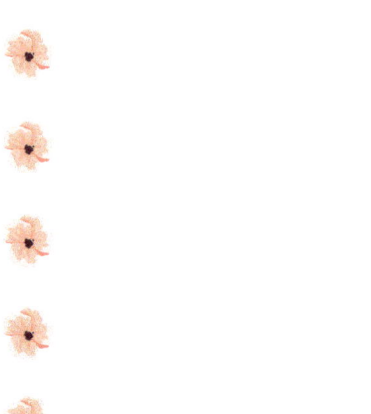

God's Whispers:

Prayer

Dear God, thank you that you do not push us away or tell us to go back to sleep, but that you welcome us and invite us closer, whether the sun is in the sky or you've hung the moon there for a time. We hear your calling and respond with a supernatural love that can only come from you. Help us to awake to our precious one's cries with renewed hope and the realization that the God of the Universe is calling us to sit at His feet with the very tiny beautiful creations He has crafted so specially for our arms, voices and eyes to connect with.
Amen.

My Prayers:

Then Eli realized that the Lord was calling the boy. So Eli told Samuel, "Go and lie down, and if he calls you, say, 'Speak, Lord, for your servant is listening.'" So Samuel went and lay down in his place.

1 Samuel 3:8b-9 (NIV)

Day 35

Pray for wisdom and read: **Ephesians 5:1-20**

Ephesians 5:15-16

Be Available

I'm not sure why, but it seems like my little ones always ask the tough questions after 9 p.m.—when bedtime has stretched beyond the hour it's supposed to, I've had my last cup of tea, and I'm ready to sit down for the first time and take a deep breath of QUIET.

Tonight my kids were apparently revolting against the human need for rest and it was pushing 10 p.m. after a full day with no naps, but I chose to lean into the Spirit who whispered, "stay," when my four-year-old held tightly to my arm and said, "Mommy, I just want you forever!"

"I just want you forever too, little buddy," I whispered, wrapping my arms around him. And just as I thought he was asleep, he rolled back over to me and asked, "Mommy, what's forgiveness?" I took a deep breath, whisper-prayed, "God, give me the right words," and did my best to explain. He was satisfied with my answer, and then went to sleep, leaving me reminded once more of the need to just BE THERE.

The big questions never come when you are expecting them or have your answers prepared. Just like when this same little man accepted Jesus in his heart in the middle of a picture book we were reading—because I paused to listen to his questions.

If you remain present, Mama, you are going to influence your babes' hearts in ways that no one else can. You have been given these precious intimate moments with these growing humans. Listen and trust that your extra efforts to BE with them, and to hear their hearts, matters in life-altering ways!

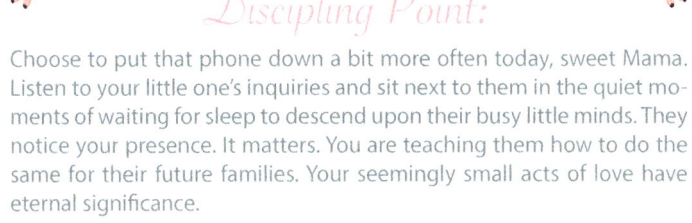

Discipling Point:

Choose to put that phone down a bit more often today, sweet Mama. Listen to your little one's inquiries and sit next to them in the quiet moments of waiting for sleep to descend upon their busy little minds. They notice your presence. It matters. You are teaching them how to do the same for their future families. Your seemingly small acts of love have eternal significance.

I am SEEN when I:

God's Whispers:

Prayer

God, thank you that I do not have to conform to the world, but that my life can look different as I choose a life centered around YOU. Help me to make wise choices about the limited time you have graced me with. Keep me present and looking into the eyes and souls of those before me.
Amen.

My Prayers:

Be very careful, then, how you live—not as unwise but as wise, making the most of every opportunity, because the days are evil.

Ephesians 5:15-16 (NIV)

Day 36

Pray for wisdom and read: **1 Chronicles 28:1-29:30**

---

1 Chronicles 29:1

Launch Your Children

Two thoughts come to mind as I read today's passage. First, Solomon is young and inexperienced, but he is CALLED by God. 1 Chronicles 28:9 (NASB) says,

> ...the Lord searches all hearts, and understands every intent of the thoughts.

God reads hearts like scholars read novels. So if God called Solomon, God knows who He is choosing to be king over Israel.

If God is calling you to something great, sweet Mama, listen. Even if you feel young and ill-equipped. If God has called you to parent that challenging child (this IS something GREAT!), don't listen to Satan's lies that you can't do it. God has called you, and you CAN do it. Lean in and love harder. Listen closer. Give more. Pray harder. Pursue his or her heart one day at a time. God will bless your faithfulness to Him and to your precious one.

Second, I see how God uses Solomon's father David to help launch him into kingship. As David aged, he wasn't out checking offt a self-focused bucket list of wants, taking fancy trips to see the world, and playing tennis in the royal courts. As you read these passages, you see that his single focus is on launching Solomon and the people into the next task to come—building a physical temple for the Lord Almighty.

David has an ETERNAL perspective here. He is fulfilling God's direction (1 Chronicles 28:2-6). He is giving all of his material goods towards the temple. He is encouraging the people to be "all in" in their giving to God. He is praying for the people's hearts and for his son's heart to stay tuned into God even once he (David) is gone from the earth. David is putting all of his final breath into breathing life into his son and God's people for generations to come. His eternal focus here moves my heart.

I pray that my husband and I spend our lives and words to the final breath to launch our kids into a life of faith…understanding that what is eternal is what matters.

Discipling Point:

Find moments today to speak God's eternal messages of hope into your kids' hearts. Call out their strengths. For example, if your child is off-the-charts curious, tell him or her, "God has really given you an extra dose of curiousity. I believe that He is going to use you to discover all kinds of ways to improve the world!" (And pray for extra patience and reminders for your own heart as you speak this truth and parent your little inquisitive engineer who dismantles random objects around your house!)

I am SEEN when I:

God's Whispers:

Prayer

God, thank you for the unique ways you have beautifully woven our family together. We certainly seem to clash at times, but I trust in your plans for GOOD, and I pray that you will direct my heart in calling out my childrens' strengths and speaking of your incredible design of each of them and your amazing plans for each of them.
Amen.

My Prayers:

Then King David said to the whole assembly: "My son Solomon, the one whom God has chosen, is young and inexperienced. The task is great, because this palatian structure is not for man but for the LORD God.

1 Chronicles 29:1 (NIV)

Day 37

Pray for wisdom and read: **John 8**

_____

_____

John 8:2

Sit Down and Teach Them, Mama

When I read today's verses, my heart immediately pictured the potential of our mornings. Note that word *potential* again there.

While we have had our picture-perfect mornings, I struggle with slow morning starts. The minute I wake, I tend to want to be accomplishing something—whether that's getting ready for the day, making breakfast, doing a Bible study or working out, it takes a lot of restraint for me to just sit on the couch and snuggle when I see baskets of laundry, the dishwasher needing unloaded, and my boys awake rubbing their always-hungry tummies that are ready for a full-course meal by 7am.

BUT we have had those sweet seasons of slower mornings. I think the infant years forced them upon me, and while feeding the babe, we would snuggle and read books before the day began. And as I was present in this capacity, we would share the sweetest unexpected learning moments together. So as I read these verses, I'm reminded of the power we hold as Mama's to set the tone for our days. When we choose to sit down amidst the chaos around us, our kids NOTICE and feel they can as well.

In our current season, this looks like me sitting down at breakfast, asking a child to pray, and reading our Bible and devotion, sometimes just getting it in before my oldest boys have scarfed down their eggs.

But I cannot emphasize enough the teaching that has come out of these "sit down" moments over the years from my kids at all ages. It doesn't take much time, but it does take persistent intention. Find what works for you, but find a sit-down moment in your day to read God's Word to your little ones, and be available to teach them God's eternal truths. Listen to the Spirit's nudgings and watch God work on all of your hearts!

Discipling Point:

Take time today to pray about your current routine of teaching your children God's Word. Are you seeing fruit in your approach? Maybe it's going great—pray for God to continue to keep your heart motivated to teach about and direct your kiddos to Him in this way! Maybe your kids are moving to older stages and need further instruction in God's Word. Take time to think about and pray for each of your children's faith journeys and realize your place in pointing them up each day.

I am SEEN when I:

God's Whispers:

Prayer

God, what an honor it is to be the one you have daily placed before my precious children. I do not take my role lightly and pray for your wisdom and leading as I awake each day in parenting them. Thank you that you are always available and whispering your direction in my ears. Help me to keep leaning in and listening.
Amen.

My Prayers:

Early in the morning He came again into the temple, and all the people were coming to Him; and He sat down and began to teach them.

John 8:2 (NASB)

Day 38

Pray for wisdom and read: **2 Samuel 22**

---

2 Samuel 22:2

Don't Drown Me Out. I Need Your Quiet. - God

I was taking a few moments to get quiet to hear God's voice recently and was feeling overwhelmed with some basic household tasks I needed to accomplish.

I felt God telling me to do those tasks, but to LISTEN to HIM while I did them. So I did. And He spoke…while I prepped dinner, while I cleaned bathrooms, while I cleaned out closets. And He affirmed that a big change was coming. One I sensed, but honestly feared and was running away from every time I felt Him speaking it to me.

He told me that if I listened to His voice, and obeyed in the little things every day, that I would be ready when the big change came. So I said yes. And then I reaaaaally wanted to tune into a podcast. And I realized that if I did so, I would drown out His voice.

I wonder how much we are drowning out God's whispers with our noise and desire (not need!) for constant stimulation. We desire the stimulation, and yet I think we NEED the quiet.

He whispered in my ear, "Don't drown me out. Everyone is trying to drown Me out! I need your quiet."

"Yes, Lord," I replied.

And so still I daily pause to listen…and quietly obey in the small tucked-in part of the world that holds my being for now. I trust that God sees me and will bless my obedience, and I trust He sees YOU and will bless your choice to pause for Him as well.

Discipling Point:

Model taking quiet time with God. Encourage your sweet ones to do the same. One year, I felt God asking me to come to Him every day and just LISTEN. I had to be strategic in grabbing my alone time, but I've managed to grab 5-10 minutes most days to quickly walk to our bedroom, throw myself across the bed and actively listen. Sometimes I make it 16.4 seconds before tiny footsteps chase me down and begin tickling my toes. Other days I've made it a full ten minutes before anyone notices my spiritual teleportaion to another realm. I tell my family I'm going to "Take Five" and they know what I'm doing. Encourage your kiddos to "Take Five" (or less time for younger ones) to listen for God's voice during a quiet time in your house.

I am SEEN when I:

God's Whispers:

Prayer

God, I long to hear your voice of direction in my life. Forgive me for drowning out your voice with things of this world. Even when they are encouraging and uplifting, remind me that nothing can take the place of quiet time at your feet. What an honor that you would pause for me. I choose to pause for you.
Amen.

My Prayers:

He said, "The Lord is my rock, my fortress and my deliverer; my God is my rock, in whom I take refuge, my shield and the horn of my salvation. He is my stronghold, my refuge and my savior—from violent people you save me.

2 Samuel 22:2-3

Day 39

Pray for wisdom and read: **1 Chronicles 21; 2 Samuel 24**

_____

_____

_____

_____

_____

2 Samuel 24:15-16a

The Angel of the Lord is Terrifying

What's your first thought when you picture an angel of God? Before studying this passage, I have to admit that our culture has infiltrated my mind to picture a beautiful, pleasant heavenly being, perhaps even blowing a trumpet or sweetly playing a harp (hello, Christmas decorations!). But according to today's reading, the Angel of the Lord came wielding a sword and struck down 70,000 men. It made five grown men hide in terror. This is no smiling cherub in a white choir robe floating around in the air.

Never forget that our God is not to be taken lightly. He is not to be turned into pretty decor to adorn our homes or catchy phrases to lighten our days. God's angel wields a sword of destruction here to show God is to be obeyed after David chooses disobedience to

God by conducting a census. We recognize that taking a census here is a sin because of Joab's reaction in 2 Sam. 24:3, and also because of David's own recognition of his sin after-the-fact (2 Samuel 24:10). While the reason this is a sin is not directly stated, we see that disobedience to God is not taken lightly here.

I write this not to discourage you, but to encourage you. When you call out to God Almighty, you call out to a power beyond the scope of your own life and your own scope of problems. His VIEW is much broader and He has POWER. Not floating robe power, but sword-smashing anger when it comes to sin and disobedience.

Let's daily make sure our hearts are in the right place with our Almighty God—and then let Him take care of the evil and injustice. He can and will. Pray with hearts aware of His POWER to change circumstances and enact justice. Align your heart with His and listen for His direction.

> *The angel of the LORD encamps around those who fear him,*
> *and he delivers them.*
> Psalm 34:7 (NIV)

 ## Discipling Point:

If you find yourself reading a children's Bible outfitted with illustrations of flowing white-robed, smiling angels, make a quick aside to your child about how God's angels are actually mighty and powerful because they work for a mighty and powerful God. You don't need to terrify young children with stories of angels striking people dead, but plant a seed in their hearts by adding just a bit more truth to the glossed-over illustrated narrative.

I am SEEN when I:

God's Whispers:

Prayer

I come before you bowed low, God, humbly realizing my position in relation to yours. I am but a passing breath here on earth, yet I long to live a life that points to your greatness and power. Thank you for the honor it is to know you and pray to you. Thank you that you choose to see and love me every day in all of my smallness. Amen.

My Prayers:

"So the Lord sent a plague on Israel from that morning until the end of the time designated, and seventy thousand of the people from Dan to Beersheba died. When the angel stretched out his hand to destroy Jerusalem, the LORD relented concerning the disaster and said to the angel who was afflicting the people, 'Enough! Withdraw your hand.'"

2 Samuel 24:15-16a

Day 40

Pray for wisdom and read: **Psalm 127**

_____

_____

Psalm 127:3

Mother for Life

There are so many different parenting narratives in this world. There are those longing for their children to stay little forever. And there are those longing for their children to grow up already.

I find myself longing for time to slow down as I giggle and enjoy my 4, 5, 8 and 10-year-old's antics. I catch myself asking them if I can put a brick on their heads to keep them little…but I am quick to tell them that I also love and long to SEE them at every age, because I am their mama FOREVER.

I've noticed that each of their faces light up when I say this. Why? Because they understand that I genuinely LOVE them as human beings and not just worship their childhood forms. What an honor it is to hold the life-long title of mother!

I firmly believe we all need people speaking truth, love, hope and encouragement into our hearts at all ages. And if we as Mama's are not actively pursuing our kids' hearts at every age to speak life into them, then who is?

Mom, God has graced you with your children. Don't take this lightly. He has entrusted you with their hearts. And just as you long for encouragement, BE that encouragement!!!

Just as God SEES you, choose to SEE and love your own children as babbling babies, SEE and love them as ornery toddlers, SEE and love them as giggling little boys and girls, SEE and love them as rapidly growing young adults, SEE and love them as adults, SEE and love them as parents and aging adults…and realize every moment is a gift. Don't wish the stages away or fear the growth—they need you to be stronger than their own fear of aging, Mama.

Pursue them with your love for life. Love never fails.

Discipling Point:

Help your children write a letter to their future selves this week, and sneak in the chance to remind them that you love them now and will love them then as well. Find moments in your days to tuck reassurances of your forever love into their hearts. Your words matter.

I am SEEN when I:

-
-
-
-
-

God's Whispers:

Prayer

God, thank you for the gift of my children! When I find myself focusing too much on the stages of life that are past, remind me of my amazing role in the present and future of my family! Keep me investing in my children's hearts, regardless of age or stage. Keep me seeing them and praying for them and loving them and pointing them to you and to loving others. Amen.

My Prayers:

Children are a gift from the LORD, they are a reward from him.

Psalm 127:3 (NLT)

Kendra Parks, author of *Grace Notes*, a best-selling Christian children's series, is a homeschooling mother of four who loves to encourage others to open up their Bibles to find God's treasures of truth for their own lives. She is grateful daily to know God and longs for you and your family to know His love.

As a little girl, she started writing out God's Word in a pocket-sized blue diary with a lock on it. She didn't realize then the power of securing God's Word into her heart. She now sees that God was planting seeds of faith that would shape her worldview, hold her up through life's challenges, and be her lifeline throughout motherhood.

She currently lives, loves, creates and writes on the edge of a whimsical forest with her best friend and husband Jason Parks (also a writer), their four brilliant dreamers, and a fluffy tail-wagging pup.

www.parkswrites.com

Other books by Kendra Parks:
Grace Notes Series

Book #1

Book #2

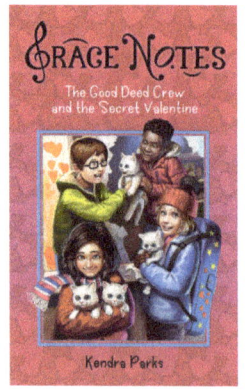
Book #3

Book #4

Book #5

The Grace Notes Children's Quartet, also known as The Good Deed Crew, wants to make a difference in their community of Tigothee Falls, Colorado, but they have promised to keep their good deeds a secret. Can these four bright and curious kids pull it off? Will the Good Deed Crew change the town without being caught?

A breath of fresh air in a world of self-focus, the *Grace Notes* series sets a new example of humility for kids today. While performing as Grace Notes—a successful traveling children's string quartet-the four young players encounter crazy fiascos and discover the needs of those around them. Under the secret name of The Good Deed Crew and with the help of Addy and Jenny's Grammy E, the kids go out of their way to fill those needs, serving and loving those in their hometown of Tigothee Falls, set in the foothills of the Rocky Mountains.

Christian author Kendra Parks has written this educational children's performing arts fiction series to bring more positive messages about humility and faith to young readers.

Additionally, Mrs. Parks draws on her own decades of experience as a musician (violinist) and teacher to make her series educational and informative about Biblical themes and classical music history.

Young Readers will learn memory verses, the names of famous composers and musical pieces, and they will see cross generational friendships. Grammy E also shares a delicious recipe to bake and enjoy at the end of each book!

Grace Notes would be an excellent series to add to your morning basket read aloud time. The chapters are short and the Christ-centered message is clear.

www.ingramcontent.com/pod-product-compliance
Lightning Source LLC
Chambersburg PA
CBHW041324110526
44592CB00021B/2811